Babylonian Epics, Hymns, Omens, and Other Texts

Ancient Texts and Translations

Series Editor
K. C. Hanson

Robert William Rogers
Cuneiform Parallels to the Old Testament

D. Winton Thomas, editor
Documents from Old Testament Times

Henry Frederick Lutz
Early Babylonian Letters from Larsa

Albert T. Clay
Babylonian Epics, Hymns, Omens, and Other Texts

Daniel David Luckenbill
The Annals of Sennacherib

A. E. Cowley
Aramaic Papyri of the Fifth Century B.C.

G. R. Driver
Aramaic Documents of the Fifth Century B.C., rev. ed.

Adolf Neubauer
The Book of Tobit

August Dillman
The Ethiopic Text of 1 Enoch

R. H. Charles
The Apocrypha and Pseudepigrapha of the Old Testament

R. H. Charles
The Book of Enoch

R. H. Charles
The Book of Jubilees

R. H. Charles
The Testaments of the Twelve Patriarchs

R. H. Charles
The Apocalypse of Baruch

H. B. Swete
The Gospel of Peter

Richard Adelbert Lipsius and Max Bonnet
Apocryphal Acts of the Apostles (3 vols.)

Babylonian
Epics, Hymns, Omens, and Other Texts

Albert T. Clay

New Bibliography by
K. C. Hanson

Wipf & Stock Publishers
Eugene, Oregon

BABYLONIAN EPICS, HYMNS, OMENS, AND OTHER TEXTS
Ancient Texts and Translations

ISBN: 1-59750-370-4

The Yale University Library has cataloged an earlier edition of this book as follows:

Clay, Albert T.
Epics, hymns, omens and other texts / edited by Albert T. Clay.

Babylonian records in the library of J. Pierpont Morgan, Pt. 4
New Haven: Yale University Press, 1923.

60 p.; 56 plates; 31 cm.

1. Assyro-Babylonian literature. 2. Epic poetry— Assyro-Babylonian. 3. Hymns—Assyro-Babylonian. 4. Omens—Assyro-Babylonian. I. Title. II. Clay, Albert T. (1866–1925).

PJ3719 M58 4

Manufactured in the U.S.A.

Series Foreword

The discoveries of documents from the ancient Near Eastern and Mediterranean worlds have altered our modern understanding of those worlds in both breadth and depth. Especially since the mid-nineteenth century, chance discoveries as well as archaeological excavations have brought to light thousands of clay tablets, stone inscriptions and stelae, leather scrolls, codices, papyri, seals, and ostraca.

The genres of these written documents are quite diverse: receipts, tax lists, inventories, letters, prophecies, blessings and curses, dowry documents, deeds, laws, instructions, collections of proverbs, philosophical treatises, state propaganda, myths and legends, hymns and prayers, liturgies and rituals, and many more. Some of them came to light in long-famous cities—such as Ur, Babylon, Nineveh, and Jerusalem—while others came from locations that were previously little-known or unknown— such as Ebla, Ugarit, Elephantine, Qumran, and Nag Hammadi.

But what good are these remnants from the distant past? Why should anyone bother with what are often fragmentary, ob-scure, or long-forgotten scraps of ancient cultures? Each person will answer those questions for herself or himself, depending upon interests and commitments. But the documents have influ-enced scholarly research in several areas.

It must first be said that the documents are of interest and importance in their own right, whatever their connections—or lack of them—to modern ethnic, religious, or ideological con-cerns. Many of them provide windows on how real people lived in the ancient world—what they grew and ate; how they related to their families, business associates, and states; how they were taxed; how and whom they worshiped; how they organized their communities; their hopes and fears; and how they understood and portrayed their own group's story.

They are of intense interest at the linguistic level. They pro-vide us with previously unknown or undeciphered languages and dialects, broaden our range of vocabularies and meanings, assist us in mapping the relationships and developments of languages, and provide examples of loan-words and linguistic influences between languages. A monumental project such as *The Assyrian Dictionary,* produced by the Oriental Institute at the University of Chicago, would have been unthinkable without the broad range of Akkadian resources today.[1] And our study of Coptic and early gospels would be impoverished without the Nag Hammadi codices.[2]

The variety of genres also attracts our interest in terms of the history of literature. Such stories as Athra-hasis, Enumma Elish, and Gilgamesh have become important to the study of world literature. While modern readers may be most intrigued by something with obvious political or religious content, we often learn a great deal from a tax receipt or a dowry document. Her-mann Gunkel influenced biblical studies not only because of his keen insights into the biblical books, but because he studied the biblical genres in the light of ancient Near Eastern texts. As he examined the genres in the Psalms, for example, he compared them to the poetic passages throughout the rest of the Bible, the Apocrypha, the Pseudepigrapha, Akkadian sources, and Egyp-tian sources.[3] While the Akkadian and Egyptian resources were much more limited in the 1920s and 1930s when he was working on the Psalms, his methodology and insights have had an on-going significance.

History is also a significant interest. Many of these texts mention kingdoms, ethnic and tribal groups, rulers, diplomats, generals, locations, or events that assist in establishing chronol-ogies, give us different perspectives on previously known events, or fill in gaps in our knowledge. Historians can never have too many sources. The Amarna letters, for example, provide us with the names of local rulers in Canaan during the fourteenth century BCE, their relationship with the pharaoh, as well as the military issues of the period.[4]

Social analysis is another area of fertile research. A deed can reveal economic structures, production, land tenure, kinship rela-tions, scribal conventions, calendars, and social hierarchies. Both the Elephantine papyri from Egypt (fifth century BCE) and the Babatha archive from the Judean desert (second century CE) include personal legal documents and letters relating to dowries, inheritance, and property transfers that provide glimpses of com-plex kinship relations, networking, and legal

---

[1] I. J. Gelb et al., editors, *The Assyrian Dictionary of the Oriental Institute of the University of Chicago* (Chicago: Univ. of Chicago Press, 1956–).

[2] James M. Robinson, editor, *The Nag Hammadi Library in English,* 3d ed. (San Francisco: HarperSanFrancisco, 1990).

[3] Hermann Gunkel, *Einleitung in die Psalmen: Die Gattungen der religiösen Lyrik Israels,* completed by Joachim Begrich, HAT (Göttingen: Vandenhoeck & Ruprecht, 1933). ET = *Introduction to the Psalms: The Genres of the Religious Lyric of Israel,* trans. James D. Nogalski, Mercer Library of Biblical Studies (Macon, Ga.: Mercer Univ. Press, 1998).

[4] William L. Moran, *The Amarna Letters* (Baltimore: Johns Hopkins Univ. Press, 1992).

witnesses.[5] And the Elephantine documents also include letters to the high priest in Jerusalem from the priests of Elephantine regarding the rebuild-ing of the Elephantine temple.

Religion in the ancient world was usually embedded in either political or kinship structures. That is, it was normally a function of either the political group or kin-group to which one belonged. We are fortunate to have numerous texts of epic literature, liturgies, and rituals. These include such things as creation stories, purification rituals, and the interpretation of sheep livers for omens. The Dead Sea Scrolls, for example, provide us with biblical books, texts of biblical interpretation, community regula-tions, and liturgical texts from the second temple period.[6]

Another key element has been the study of law. A variety of legal principles, laws, and collections of regulations provide windows on social structures, economics, governance, property rights, and punishments. The stele of Hammurabi of Babylon (c. 1700 BCE) is certainly the most famous. But we have many more, for example: Ur-Nammu (c. 2100 BCE), Lipit-Ishtar (c. 1850 BCE), and the Middle Assyrian Laws (c. 1150 BCE).

The intention of Ancient Texts and Translations (ATT) is to make available a variety of ancient documents and document collections to a broad range of readers. The series will include reprints of long out-of-print volumes, revisions of earlier editions, and completely new volumes. The understanding of an-cient societies depends upon our close reading of the documents, however fragmentary, that have survived.

—K. C. Hanson
Series Editor

---

[5] Bezalel Porten et al., editors, *The Elephantine Papyri in English: Three Millennia of Cross-Cultural Continuity and Change,* Documenta et Monumenta Orientis Antiqui 22 (Leiden: Brill, 1996); Yigael Yadin et al., *The Finds from the Bar Kokhba Period in the Cave of Letters,* 3 vols., Judean Desert Studies (Jerusalem: Israel Exploration Society, 1963–2002) [NB: vols. 2 and 3 are titled *Documents* instead of *Finds*].

[6] Florentino Garcia Martinez, *The Dead Sea Scrolls Translated: The Qumran Texts in English,* 2d ed., trans. Wilfred G. E. Watson (Grand Rapids: Eerdmans, 1996).

Select Bibliography

A. Diverse Collections

Beyerlin, Walter, editor. *Near Eastern Religious Texts Relating to the Old Testament.* Translated by John Bowden. Old Testament Library. Philadelphia: Westminster, 1978.

Hallo, William W., and K. Lawson Younger Jr., editors. *The Context of Scripture.* Vol. 1: *Canonical Compositions from the Biblical World.* Leiden: Brill, 1997.

———. *The Context of Scripture.* Vol. 2: *Monumental Inscriptions from the Biblical World.* Leiden: Brill, 1999.

———. *The Context of Scripture.* Vol. 3: *Archival Documents from the Biblical World.* Leiden: Brill, 2002.

Matthews, Victor H., and Don C. Benjamin. *Old Testament Parallels.* 2d ed. New York: Paulist, 1997.

Pritchard, James B., editor. *Ancient Near Eastern Texts Relating to the Old Testament.* 3d ed. Princeton: Princeton Univ. Press, 1969.

Thomas, D. Winton, editor. *Documents from Old Testament Times.* Ancient Texts and Translations. Eugene, Ore.: Wipf & Stock, 2005.

B. Akkadian

Beaulieu, Paul-Alain. *Legal and Administrative Texts from the Reign of Nabonidus.* Yale Oriental Series: Babylonian Texts 1. New Haven: Yale Univ. Press,

Beckman, Gary. *Old Babylonian Archival Texts in the Yale Babylonian Collection.* Catalogue of the Babylonian Collections at Yale 4. Bethesda, Md.: CDL, 2000.

Bergmann, E., et al., editors. *Codex Hammurabi.* 3d ed. 2 vols. Pontificio Instituto Biblico Scripta 51. Rome: Pontifical Biblical Institute, 1950–53.

Biggs, Robert D. *Šà.zi.ga: Ancient Mesopotamian Potency Incantations.* Texts from Cuneiform Sources 2. Locust Valley, N.Y.: Augustin, 1967.

Clay, Albert T. *Miscellaneous Inscriptions in the Yale Babylonian Collection.* Yale Oriental Series: Babylonian Texts 1. New Haven: Yale Univ. Press, 1915.

———. *Neo-Babylonian Letters from Erech.* Yale Oriental Series: Babylonian Texts 3. New Haven: Yale Univ. Press, 1919.

———. *A Hebrew Deluge Story in Cuneiform: And Other Epic Fragments in the Pierpont Morgan Library.* Yale Oriental Series: Researches 3. New Haven: Yale Univ. Press, 1922.

Cole, Steven W., and Peter Machinist, editors. *Letters from Priests to the Kings Esarhaddon and Assurbanipal.* State Archives of Assyria 13. Helsinki: Helsinki Univ. Press, 1998.

Dalley, Stephanie. *Myths from Mesopotamia.* Oxford: Oxford Univ. Press, 1989.

———. *Old Babylonian Texts in the Ashmolean Museum: Texts from Kish and Elsewhere.* Oxford Editions of Cuneiform Texts 13. Oxford: Clarendon, 1991.

Dijk, Jan van, editor. *Texts in the Iraq Museum.* 9 vols. Leiden: Brill, 1964–.

———, Albrecht Goetze, and Mary I. Hussey. *Early Mesopotamian Incantations and Rituals.* Yale Oriental Series: Babylonian Texts 11. New Haven: Yale Univ. Press, 1985.

Dossin, Georges, and André Parrot, editors. *Archives Royales de Mari: Textes.* Paris: Geuthner, 1942–.

Dougherty, Raymond Philip. *Records from Erech: Time of Nabonidus (555–538 B. C.).* Yale Oriental Series: Babylonian Texts 6. New Haven: Yale Univ. Press, 1920.

Driver, G. R. *Letters of the First Babylonian Dynasty.* Oxford Editions of Cuneiform Texts 3. Oxford: Clarendon, 1924.

———, and John C. Miles. *The Assyrian Laws.* Ancient Codes and Laws of the Near East. Oxford: Clarendon, 1935.

———, and John C. Miles. *The Babylonian Laws.* Rev. ed. 2 vols. Ancient Codes and Laws of the Near East. Oxford: Clarendon, 1960–68.

Fales, F. M., and J. N. Postgate, editors. *Imperial Administrative Records.* State Archives of Assyria 7. Helsinki: Helsinki Univ. Press, 1992–.

Faust, David Earl. *Contracts from Larsa, Dated in the Reign of Rim-Sin.* Yale Oriental Series: Babylonian Texts 8. New Haven: Yale Univ. Press, 1941.

Foster, Benjamin R. *Before the Muses: An Anthology of Akkadian Literature.* 3d ed. Bethesda, Md.: CDL, 2005.

———. *From Distant Days: Myths, Tales and Poetry from Ancient Mesopotamia.* Bethesda, Md.: CDL, 1995.

———, Douglas Frayne, and Gary Beckman. *The Epic of Gilgamesh: A New Translation, Analogues, Criticism.* Norton Critical Edition. New York: Norton, 2001.

Gelb, I. J. *Sargonic Texts from the Diyala Region.* Materials for the Assyrian Dictionary 1. Chicago: Univ. of Chicago, 1952.

———. *Old Akkadian Inscriptions in Chicago Natural History Museum.* Chicago Natural History Museum, Anthropology 44.2. Chicago: Texts of Legal and Business Interests, 1955.

———. *Sargonic Texts in the Ashmolean Museum, Oxford.* Materials for the Assyrian Dictionary 5. Chicago: Univ. of Chicago, 1970.

———. *Sargonic Texts in the Louvre Museum.* Materials for the Assyrian Dictionary 4. Chicago: Univ. of Chicago, 1970.

———, et al., editors. *Assyrian Dictionary of the Oriental Institute of the University of Chicago.* Chicago: Oriental Institute, 1956–.

George, A. R. *The Babylonian Gilgamesh Epic: Introduction, Critical Edition, and Cuneiform Texts.* 2 vols. Oxford: Oxford Univ. Press, 2003.

Glassner, Jean-Jacques. *Mesopotamian Chronicles.* Writings from the Ancient World 19. Atlanta: Society of Biblical Literature, 2004.

Goetze, Albrecht. *Old Babylonian Omen Texts.* Yale Oriental Series: Babylonian Texts 10. New Haven: Yale Univ. Press, 1947.

———. *The Laws of Eshnunna.* Annual of the American Schools of Oriental Research 31. New Haven: Dept. of Antiquities of the Government of Iraq and the American Schools of Oriental Research, 1956.

Grayson, A. Kirk. *Assyrian and Babylonian Chronicles.* Texts from Cuneiform Sources 5. Locust Valley, N.Y.: Augustin, 1970.

———. *Assyrian Royal Inscriptions.* 2 vols. Records of the Ancient Near East. Wiesbaden: Harrassowitz, 1972–.

———. *Babylonian Historical-Literary Texts.* Toronto Semitic Texts and Studies 3. Toronto: Univ. of Toronto Press, 1975.

———. *Assyrian Rulers of the Third and Second Millennia BC (to 1115 BC).* Royal Inscriptions of Mesopotamia: Assyrian Periods 1. Toronto: Univ. of Toronto Press, 1987.

———. *Assyrian Rulers of the Early First Millennium BC I (1114–859 BC).* Royal Inscriptions of Mesopotamia: Assyrian Periods 2. Toronto: Univ. of Toronto Press, 1991.

Gurney, O. R. *The Middle Babylonian Legal and Economic Texts from Ur.* Oxford: Alden, 1983.

———. *Literary and Miscellaneous Texts in the Ashmolean Museum.* Oxford Editions of Cuneiform Texts 11. Oxford: Clarendon, 1989.

———, and J. J. Finkelstein. *The Sultantepe Tablets.* 2 vols. Occasional Publications of the British Institute of Archaeology at Ankara 3. London: British Institute of Archaeology at Ankara, 1957–64.

Hinke, W. J. *Selected Babylonian Kudurru Inscriptions.* Semitic Study Series 14. Leiden: Brill, 1911.

Hunger, Hermann, editor. *Astrological Reports to Assyrian Kings.* State Archives of Assyria 8. Helsinki: Helsinki Univ. Press, 1992.

Jastrow, Morris Jr., and Albert T. Clay. *An Old Babylonian Version of the Gilgamesh Epic: On the Basis of Recently Discovered Texts.* Yale Oriental Series: Researches 4.3. New Haven: Yale Univ. Press, 1920.

Johannès, Francis. *Neo-Babylonian Tablets in the Ashmolean Museum.* Oxford Editions of Cuneiform Texts 12. Oxford: Clarendon, 1990.

Kataja, L., and R. Whiting, editors. *Grants, Decrees and Gifts of the Neo-Assyrian Period.* State Archives of Assyria 12. Helsinki: Helsinki Univ. Press, 1995.

Kwasman, Theodore, and Simo Parpola, editors. *Legal Transactions of the Royal Court of Nineveh.* 2 vols. State Archives of Assyria 6, 14. Helsinki: Helsinki Univ. Press, 1991–2002.

Lambert, W. G. *Babylonian Wisdom Literature.* Oxford: Clarendon, 1960.

Lau, Robert J., and Stephen Langdon. *The Annals of Ashurbanipal (V Rawlinson pl. I-X).* Semitic Study Series 2. Leiden: Brill, 1903.

Leichty, Erle. *The Omen Series summa izbu.* Texts from Cuneiform Sources 4. Locust Valley, N.Y.: Augustin, 1970.

Livingstone, Alasdair, editor. *Court Poetry and Literary Miscellanea.* State Archives of Assyria 3. Helsinki: Helsinki Univ. Press, 1989.

Luckenbill, Daniel David. *The Annals of Sennacherib.* University of Chicago Oriental Institute Publications 2. Chicago: Univ. of Chicago Press, 1924.

———. *Ancient Records of Assyria and Babylonia.* 2 vols. Chicago: Univ. of Chicago Press, 1926–27.

Lutz, Henry Frederick. *Early Babylonian Letters from Larsa.* Yale Oriental Series: Babylonian Texts 2. New Haven: Yale Univ. Press, 1917.

Luukko, Mikko, and Greta van Buylaere, editors. *The Political Correspondence of Esarhaddon.* State Archives of Assyria 16. Helsinki: Helsinki Univ. Press, 2002.

McEwan, Gilbert J. P. *Late Babylonian Texts in the Ashmolean Museum.* Oxford Editions of Cuneiform Texts 10. Oxford: Clarendon, 1984.

Mercer, Samuel A. B. *The Tell Amarna Tablets.* 2 vols. Toronto: Macmillan, 1939.

Michalowski, Piotr. *Letters from Early Mesopotamia.* Writings from the Ancient World 3. Atlanta: Scholars, 1993.

Moran, William L. *The Amarna Letters.* Baltimore: Johns Hopkins Univ. Press, 1992.

Murnane, William J. *Texts from the Amarna Period in Egypt.* Writings from the Ancient World 5. Atlanta: Scholars, 1995.

Neugebauer, Otto. *Mathematische Keilschrift-Texte.* 3 vols. in 2. Quellen und Studien zur Geschichte der Mathematik, Astronomie und Physik 3. Berlin: Springer, 1935–37.

Nissinen, Martti. *Prophets and Prophecy in the Ancient Near East.* Writings from the Ancient World 12. Atlanta: Society of Biblical Literature, 2003.

Parpola, Simo. *Letters from Assyrian Scholars to the Kings Esarhaddon and Assurbanipal.* 2 vols. Alter Orient und Altes Testament 5/1-2. Kevelaer: Butzon & Bercker, 1970–83.

———. *The Correspondence of Sargon II.* 3 vols. State Archives of Assyria 1, 5, 15. Helsinki: Helsinki Univ. Press, 1987–2001.

———. *Neo-Assyrian Treaties and Loyalty Oaths.* State Archives of Assyria 2. Helsinki: Helsinki Univ. Press, 1988.

———. *Letters from Assyrian and Babylonian Scholars.* State Archives of Assyria 10. Helsinki: Helsinki Univ. Press, 1993.

———. *Assyrian Prophecies.* State Archives of Assyria 9. Helsinki: Helsinki Univ. Press, 1997.

Piepkorn, Arthur Carl. *Historical Prism Inscriptions of Ashurbanipal.* Assyriological Studies 5. Chicago: Univ. of Chicago Press, 1933.

Pinches, T. G., et al. *Late Babylonian Astronomical and Related Texts.* Brown University Studies 18. Providence: Brown Univ. Press, 1955.

Rawlinson, H. C. *A Selection from the Miscellaneous Inscriptions of Assyria and Babylonia.* Cuneiform Inscriptions of Western Asia 5. London: Harrison, 1909.

Reynolds, Frances. *The Babylonian Correspondence of Esarhaddon, and Letters to Assurbanipal and Sin-Sarru-Iskun from Northern and Central Babylonia.* State Archives of Assyria 18. Helsinki: Helsinki Univ. Press, 2003.

Robson, Eleanor. *Mesopotamian Mathematics, 2100–1600 BC: Technical Constants in Bureaucracy and Education.* Oxford Editions of Cuneiform Texts 14. New York: Clarendon, 1998.

Starr, Ivan. *Queries to the Sungod: Divination and Politics in Sargonid Assyria.* State Archives of Assyria 4. Helsinki: Helsinki Univ. Press, 1990.

Stephens, Ferris J. *Votive and Historical Texts from Babylonia and Assyria.* Yale Oriental Series: Babylonian Texts 9. New Haven: Yale Univ. Press, 1937.

Tadmor, Hayyim. *The Inscriptions of Tiglath-pileser III, King of Assyria: Critical Edition, with Introductions, Translations, and Commentary.* Publications of the Israel Academy of Sciences and Humanities, Section of Humanities. Jerusalem: Israel Academy of Sciences and Humanities, 1994.

Thompson, R. Campbell. *Assyrian Medical Texts from the Originals in the British Museum.* London: Oxford Univ. Press, 1923.

Tremayne, Arch. *Records from Erech: Time of Cyrus and Cambyses (538–521 B.C.).* Yale Oriental Series: Babylonian Texts 7. New Haven: Yale Univ. Press, 1925.

Weisberg, David B. *Texts from the Time of Nebuchadnezzar.* Yale Oriental Series: Babylonian Texts 17. New Haven: Yale Univ. Press, 1980.

Whiting, Robert M. *Old Babylonian Letters from Tell Asmar.* Assyriological Studies 22. Chicago: Oriental Institute, 1987.

Yaron, Reuven. *The Laws of Eshnunna.* Jerusalem: Magnes, 1969.

CONTENTS

INTRODUCTION

INTRODUCTION.

This series is mainly intended to make the cuneiform inscriptions of the Library accessible to scholars. In addition to the texts and indices, however, the transliteration and translation of many of the texts are also offered. Several of the inscriptions were published years ago in the conventional Assyrian script, or simply in transliteration, before these came into the possession of the Library. They are included here because, besides other reasons, further study of the originals has made it possible to improve readings. The first three inscriptions of this volume were recently published by the writer in *A Hebrew Deluge Story in Cuneiform and Other Epic Fragments in the Pierpont Morgan Library*.

No. 1. Early Dated Hebrew Deluge Story.

About twenty-five years ago this fragment of a large tablet was published in text, transliteration, and translation; since which time also many other translations and discussions of it have appeared.[1] On further study it proves to be an ancient version of a Hebrew or Amorite deluge story, or what might be called The Atra-ḫasis Epic. The so-called Ea and Atra-ḫasis Epic proves to be a late redaction of it, which was used for incantation purposes.

The scribe who copied this ancient version from a still earlier inscription was named Azag-Aya. He dated his work on the 28th day of Shebet, in the 11th year of Ammi-zaduga (1966 B. C.); in other words, this tablet was written about 1300 years prior to the time of Ashurbanipal (668–626 B. C.), in whose Library the late redaction of it was found. It is the only dated deluge story that has been discovered.

[1] Scheil *Recueil de Travaux* 20 (1898), 55 ff; Jensen *KB* VI 1 288 ff; Dhorme *Choix de Textes Religieux Assyro-Babyloniens* 120 ff; Ungnad *ATB* I, 57 f; Rogers *Cuneiform Parallels* 104 ff, etc.

The series, of which this fragment is a part of the second tablet, was entitled, *i-nu-ma i-lu a-we-lum* "When God, man."[1] For the transliteration, translation, and discussion of the text by the present writer, see *A Hebrew Deluge Story in Cuneiform and other Epic Fragments in the Pierpont Morgan Library.* (*YOR* V, 3.)

No. 2. An Ancient Version of the Etana Legend.

The legend of Etana and the Eagle has also been handed down in a fragmentary condition. All the fragments known of this legend, except the present one, have come from the library in Nineveh, and were written in the Assyrian period.[2] The text here published was written much earlier, which for palæographical reasons must be assigned to a period about 1700 years prior to Ashurbanipal's time. The text was previously published in the conventional script of the late Assyrian period.[3] The present text, however, is copied in the script of the tablet, and offers additional lines and characters not hitherto presented.

The fragment contains the opening and the closing lines of a large tablet, which had three columns on the obverse, and three on the reverse. It seems to the writer that the complete tablet must have contained about 275 lines. Among the fragments of the epic written in the Assyrian period there is one which duplicates partially some lines of the present text. The transliteration, translation, and discussion of this text is also found in *A Hebrew Deluge Story*, 33 ff.

No. 3. The Legend of Adapa.

What is known of the Legend of Adapa is based upon several fragmentary tablets which at one time also belonged to the Library of

[1] This title was read heretofore *i-nu-ma ṣal-lu a-we-lum* "when a man lay down to sleep," but this is incorrect.

[2] George Smith *Chaldean Genesis* 138 ff, published the first three known fragments. E. J. Harper published seven other fragments *BA* II, 441 ff and 503 ff; Jastrow *BA* III, 379 ff and *AJSL* 30, 101 ff published two others. See Jensen *KB* VI 1, 100 ff.

[3] Scheil *Recueil de Travaux* 23, 18 ff. A transliteration and translation on the basis of the same text was published by Jensen *KB* VI 1, 100 ff; and 581 ff. See also Frank *Studien zur Babylonischen Religion* 105 ff.

Ashurbanipal,[1] including the present text,[2] and upon one that was found among the Egyptian archives of Amenophis III and IV, of the fourteenth century B. C.[3] The present fragment contains the first part of the legend. For the transliteration, translation, and dicsussion see *A Hebrew Deluge Story* (39 ff).

No. 4. Inscription of Sargon (c. 2830 B. C.).

It would seem that the fragment of a tablet containing the lines which follow, belonged to the ruler commonly referred to as Sargon I, the founder of the Kish-Akkad dynasty. It is to be regretted that the tablet is not complete.

A-na-ku Ša-ru-ki-in[4]	I Sargon,
na-ra-am [d]*Ištar*	the beloved of Ishtar,
mu-te-li-ik	the ruler(?)
ki-ib-ra-at	of the four
ir-bi-ti-in	quarters,
.....*mi(?)-ta-ru-ru*	......

No. 5. Label which Accompanied a Royal Gift.

The little tablet probably accompanied a gift sent by the king to a lady named Shaggamu. It would seem from the script that it was written in the middle of the third millennium B. C. Its provenance may be Jokha, the ancient Umma, or Drehem, as it was found among tablets from these two sites. This Sumerian inscription reads:

Šag-ga-mu	To Shaggamu,
dam Gimil-Nin-Šubur-ra	the wife of Gimil-Nin-Shubur,
lugal-e	the king
šu-in-ni-in-ba	has presented it.
dub sukal-maḫ	Tablet of the Chief Messenger.

[1] See *K.* 8219, published by Strong *PSBA* 16, 274 f; and *K.* 8743, published by Jensen *KB* VI 1, XVII ff.

[2] This text and its translation were originally published by Scheil, *Recueil de Travaux* 20 (1898), 127 ff. Zimmern from a photograph, in Gunkel *Schöpfung und Chaos* 420 ff, offered several improved readings. These were utilized by Jensen *KB* VI 1, 92 ff, as well as by others. For other translations see Ungnad *ATB* I, 34 ff; Rogers *Cuneiform Parallels* 67 ff; Barton *Archæology and the Bible* 260 ff; and Langdon *UMBS* X 1, 38 ff.

[3] See Winckler and Abel *Thontafelfund von El-Amarna* No. 240; and Schröder *VS* 12, 194. For the transliteration and translation see Knudtzon *Die El-Amarna Tafeln* No. 356, p. 964 ff.

[4] The name of Sargon has been written *Šar-ru-ki-in* (Scheil *C R*, 1911, 606 ff); *Šar-ru-kîn(GI)* (Poebel *HT* VI 1 p. 187); *Šar-um-kîn(GI) ibid.* p 176; *Šarru-ukîna* (*GI-na, GIN*) King *Chron* II p. 2, 25, etc.; and the above. A translation of this text first appeared in the writer's *Amurru* p. 194.

No. 6. Ritual for the Observance of Eclipses.

Among the multitude of reports of the magicians and astrologers discovered in the Library of Ashurbanipal, as well as omens, it is ascertained that eclipses figured prominently in the prognostications of the Babylonian seer. Among the forecasts in the event of eclipses occurring at certain times, famines, plagues, inundations, etc., were supposed to ensue. The present text belonged to the temple ritual, and contains directions for the proper observance of eclipses. The colophon is wanting; but it presumably belonged to the temple ritual at Erech; and was written in the Seleucid era.[1]

Transliteration.

. . . . u ra- . . . .

[$^{am\bar{e}l}$kalû ku-um-ma] ni-piš ša qât $^{am\bar{e}l}$kalû ša-ṭar u . . . .

. . zi ṣi-si-tu ultu bi-it ^{d}Nikkal zin-niš-tum ša ^{d}[En-zu] . . . .

. . -tum um-mu ^{d}Nikkal ina a-lu it-ta-ṣi

[ardi]-ka ša i-dul-lu-ma la i-ṣa-al-lal ana-ku

[ša ina ma]-na-aḫ-ti-šu a-kal la i-kul ana-ku ša ina ma-na-aḫ-ti-šu me-e la iš-tu-ú ana-ku

. . . a-ba-az it-taš-pak i-pi-ir it-ta-bak kab-tu ša di-im-ma-at da-ma-ma ul i-kal-lu

[ša ina muḫ]-ḫi âli-šu ru-bu-ú ina qaq-qar na-bal-si-iḫ me-ḫu-ú it-ba-am i-pi-ir pa-ni ik-tu-mu

[û-m]u a-mat ^{d}Anu û-mu a-mat ^{d}En-lil û-mu ug-ga-at lib-bi ša ^{d}Anu ra-bi-i

. . -mun-nu-u ša ina ṣu-ṣi-e e-lul-šu it-bu-ú ana-ku

ša lib-bi i-šu-ú u e-mu-qu la i-šu-ú ana-ku ⁝ ú-a lib-bi ú-a ka-bat-ta

ma-kur-ru ša nin-da-bu-ú iz-bil ta-ni-iḫ iz-za-bil

ša nin-da-bi-e nin-da-bi-e ul u-še-rib ⁝ ša ni-qa-a ni-qa-a ul ú-še-rib

an-na-a ša a-na ^{d}Sin ina attalî iz-za-mir ⁝ ina bâbi bît ilâni$^{me\check{s}}$ u rîbâti ga-rak-ku inamdi(-di)

^{iṣ}erina ^{iṣ}surmêna âsa aba ṭâba bîna šadâ u lu-te-e ^{iṣ}eru ina muḫ-ḫi ga-rak-ku te-ṣi-en

ki-ma attalî u-ša-ru-ú $^{am\bar{e}l}$TU-E ṭipâra(GI-BIL-LÁ) i-qa-da-ma it-ti ga-rak-ku ú-ša-aṣ-ba-at

[1] I am indebted to my former colleague, the late Professor Jastrow, for a number of suggestions in connection with this and several texts which follow.

^{amêl}*kalû ku-um-ma ni-piš ša qât* ^{amêl}*kalû a-di attalî u-nam-mir ippuš (-uš)*

a-di attalî u-nam-mar išâti ina muḫ-ḫi ga-rak-ku la te-bil

ki-is-pi a-na ugarê(A-KAR-RU)^{meš} *ta-kas-sap ki-is-pi a-na narâti*^{meš} *ša me-e la ub-bal KI-MIN*

ki-is-pi a-na ^{d}*A-nun-na-ki ta-kas-sap*

a-di attalî u-nam-mar nišê^{meš} *mâti ṣu-bat qaqqadi-šu-nu ittaššû (GAR.ÎL) ina lu-bar-ra-šu-nu qaqqad-su-nu kat-mu*

sib-bu ner-ti bar-tum u attalî ai it-ḫu-u a-na Uruk^{ki} *bît ri-eš eš-gal parmaḫḫu E-an-na*

u bîtâti^{meš} *ilâni*^{meš} ^{d}*Tir-an-na*^{ki} *i-ša-as-su-ú a-na ṣi-ri-iḫ-ti ri-gim-šu-nu i-nam-du-ú*

7 ^{amêl}*ṣabâni(-ni) nišê*^{meš} *ma-a-tu im-ki šub-tu nâru inê*^{meš}*-šu-nu qâtâ*^{meš}*-šu-nu u šepâ-šu-nu pa-aš-šu*

paṭru ina gir-ri imni-šu-nu ta-al-lal

šib-bu ner-ti bar-tum u attalî ai it-hu-ú a-na Uruk^{ki} *bît ri-eš eš-gal parmaḫḫu E-an-na*

ù bîtâti^{meš} *ilâni*^{meš} ^{d}*Tir-an-na*^{ki} *i-ša-as-su-u a-na ṣi-ri-iḫ-ti ri-gim-šu-nu i-nam-du-ú*

a-di attalî i-zak-ku-u i-ša-as-su-ú ⁑ *ki-ma ša* ^{d}*Sin attalî u-nam-mar*

išâti ina muḫ-ḫi ga-rak-ku ina BI-MAT-NAM tu-kab-bat

ina šanî(-i) û-mu ^{amêl}*bânû ga-rak-ku a-di di-iq-me-en-šu ittaš-ši (ÎL-ši)-ma a-na nâri inamdi (-di)*

---

ina šanî(-i) û-mu la-am ^{d}*Šamaš nap-ḫa bâbâni*^{meš} *ša tu-kan-nak pit-te uru-gallûtu(NAM-SIS-GAL) ku-sur-ra-a*

^{ṣubât}*ú-li-nu piṣu-ú u ṣalmu tu-rab-ba a-na nâri tanamdi(-di) tak-pi-ra-at bîtâti*^{meš} *ilâni*^{meš} *kalama(KAK-A-BI)*

ù E-tur-nun-na bît ^{d}*Sin tu-kap-par* ^{d}*Sin KU-KU karpati a-li-ba uk-tan-nu*

ZI ^{d}Anu ^{d}Enlil me(?)-bi ḫe-pad-da-eš ⁑ *niš* ^{d}*A-num u* ^{d}*Enlil tum-mu-šu-nu-ti*

išten(-en) ^{amêl}*mašmašu imni bîti ù ša-nu-ú šumêli bîti šipta* ud-ud-du-a-meš *šit-nu-ú*

ù šit-ti ^{amêl}*mašmašê*^{meš} *šipta* gidim ḫul-meš *šit-nu-ú niš* pa-di-e-meš *u-ta-am-mu-ú-šu-nu-ti*

ina šanî(-i) û-mu ku-sur-ra-a tak-pi-rat ù ga-rak-ku ana nâri tunamdi(-di)

ša-niš ina û-mu attalî ^{d}Sin ^{amêl}šangû^{meš} ša bîtâti^{meš} ilâni^{meš} Tir-an-na^{ki} ina bâbi bîti ilâni^{meš}-šu-nu ga-rak-ku inamdû(di-ú)
nu-ur ú-ša-aṣ-bat šib-bu ner-ti maš-tum u attalû ai it-ḫu-ú â-na Uruk^{ki} bît ri-eš eš-gal
parmaḫḫi E-an-na ù bîtâti^{meš} ilâni^{meš} Tir-an-na^{ki} i-ša-as-su-ú
a-na ṣi-ri-iḫ-ti ri-gim-šu-nu i-nam-du-ú a-di attalî i-zaq-ku-ú i-ša-as-su-ú
û-mu attalî ^{d}Sin ḫal-ḫal-lat siparru eršemma siparru lilissu siparru ištu bîti am-mu-uš mu-íl-lam-ma
it-ti bara-ki-dúb *ša ili ki-ma ša attalî ^{d}Sin šanû(-ú) ^{amêl}kalê^{meš} ṣabitu ^{kitû}litbušu(KU-KU)*
ina lu-bar-šu-nu nu-uk-su-tu qaqqad-su-(šu-)nu kat-mu ṣi-ri-iḫ-tu ni-iṣ-sa-ti u bi-ki-ti
a-na ^{d}Sin ina attalî na-šu-ú 3 ^{subât}DUB-DUB-BU a-na mi-iḫ-rat lilissi ina ku-sur-ra-a tanamdi(-di)
išten(-en) ku-uk-ku-bu di-im-ti ša SINIG(?) qu-ud-du-uš me-e ina zak-ku ^{subât}DUB-DUB-BU šelalti-šu-nu
ina ku-sur-ra-a a-na kun-nu qât a-na ^{amêl}kalê^{meš} a-na mi-iḫ-rat ^{d}Sin ina attalî tušakan(-an)
ki-i šal-šu si-rat ši-kin attalî rîmu supûru(AMAS-NA) ša ^{d}Me-ir-me-ir napišti(ZI) itakkal(KU-E) a-na lib-bi i-ru-bu
a-zu-ab-mu mu-un-ḫul-am ír meze-ma ⁂ *ki-i 2-ta-qât si-rat ši-kin attalî rîmu supûri(AMAS-NA)*
'u-ú-a a-šag-zu gar-an ù a-zu-ab-mu mu-un-[ḫul-am *^{d}Me]-ir-me-ır napišti(ZI) itakkal(KU-E)*
ki-i mit-mar-tum ṣiḫru-tim ši(?)-kin(?) attalî rîmi supûru(AMAS-NA)....tušakan(-an)
'u-ú-a a-šàg-[zu..................*supûru(AMAS-NA)*
an-na................

Translation.

[the *kalû* priest at the place] for the service by the hand of the *kalû*, the writing.....
...from the temple of Nikkal the wife of [Sin].....
...mother, Nikkal from the city went forth;
thy [servant] who works, and does not rest, am I;
[who in] his resting place, ate no food, am I; who in his resting place, drank no water, am I;

. . . he pours out; covers himself with dust; the honored one, who does not hold back tears of lament.

Who, over his city is a prince, who prostrates himself upon the ground; when a storm arises, covers the face with dirt.

A storm (?) by the word of Anu, a storm by the word of Enlil, a storm by the wrath of the heart of Anu, the great,

. . . . which he bound (?) in the marsh, came on, am I.

The one who has courage; but strength he has not, am I. Sorrow of heart, sorrow of liver.

A wealth of offerings he has brought, lamentation he has brought.

As regards offerings, offerings he did not bring; as regards libations, libations he did not bring.

This is that which to Sin during an eclipse he shall sing. In the gate of the house of the gods, and in the wide places, he shall place an altar (*garakku*).

Cedar, cypress, myrtle, good reed, mountain tamarisk(?), and a cedar *lutû*, upon the *garakku* thou shalt heap up.

As the eclipse begins, the *TU-E* priest shall light the torch, and attach it to the *garakku*.

The *kalû* priest, at the place for the service by the hand of the *kalû*, as long as the eclipse has lasted, shall perform.

As long as the eclipse lasts, the fire upon the *garakku* thou shalt not remove.

A dirge for the fields thou shalt intone; a dirge for the streams that the water shall not devastate, thou shalt intone.

A dirge to the Anunnaki thou shalt intone.

As long as the eclipse lasts, the people of the land shall remove their headgear; they shall cover their heads with their garments.

That catastrophe, murder, rebellion, and the eclipse approach not unto Erech, Bit-rêsh, Eshgal the shrine of E-anna,

and the houses of the gods of Tiranna, they shall cry aloud; for a lamentation they shall send up their cry.

Seven workmen of the people of the country, the family, the dwelling, the river, their eyes, their hands and their feet, shall be anointed.

The dagger in the sheath shall hang on their right side.

That catastrophe, murder, rebellion, and the eclipse shall not approach unto Erech, Bît-rêsh, Eshgal, the shrine of Eanna, and the houses of the gods of Tiranna, they shall cry aloud. For a lamentation they shall send up their cry.

Until the eclipse is past, they shall shout. As soon as the moon appears from the eclipse,

the fire upon the *garakku*, with the *BI-MAT-NAM*, thou shalt extinguish.

On the second day, the builder shall remove the *garakku*, including its ashes, and throw into the river.

On the second day, before the sun arises, the gates which thou sealest, open. The *uru-gallutu* of the *kusurra*,

with a white and black garment, thou shalt wrap; into the river thou shalt throw. The purification of the houses of all the gods

and E-tur-nunna, the house of the god Sin, thou shalt perform. As regards the moon, a *KU-KU* pot of milk they shall set.

By Anu and Enlil conjure them.

One magician on the right of the house, and a second on the left of the house, shall repeat the incantation **Ud-uddu-a-mesh**

And two magicians shall repeat the incantation **Gidim-ḫul-mesh.** By the **Pa-di-e-mesh,** they shall conjure them.

On the second day, the *kusurra*, the purification mass, and the *garakku* thou shalt throw into the river.

Again, on the day of the eclipse of the moon, the priests of the houses of the gods of Tir-anna shall place a *garakku* in the gate of the house of their gods.

When the light fails, that catastrophe, murder, rebellion, and the eclipse approach not upon Erech, Bît-rêsh, Eshgal,

the shrine of E-anna, and the houses of the gods of Tir-anna, they shall cry aloud.

For a lamentation they shall regard their cry. Until the eclipse is past, they shall cry aloud.

On the day of the eclipse of the moon, the copper *ḫallallat,* the copper *ershemma*, the copper *lilissu*, from the house, the **Am-mu-us mu-il-lam-ma**

with **Bara-ki-dúb** of the god, like at the eclipse of the moon are repeated; the *kalû* priests, clothed in a linen garment,

with a short garment thrown over their head, a lamentation of grief and weeping to the eclipsed moon shall raise. Three *dubdubbu* garments in front of the *lilissu*, in the *kusurru*, thou shalt place.

One jar of *binu dimti*, holy water for the purification of their three *dubdubbu* garments,

in the *kusurra*, for steadying (?) the hand of the *kalû* priests, thou shalt place in the view of the moon during the eclipse.

If a third ring (?) is a feature of a deep eclipse, the halo of Mermer shall consume the *ZI*, as into it they enter,

A-zu-ab-mu mu-un-ḫul-am ír meze-ma (shall be repeated). If 2 rings (?) are a feature of the eclipse, the halo of Mermer shall consume the *ZI*,

'u-ú-a a-šàg-zu gar-an and **a-zu-ub-mu mu-un-ḫul-am** (shall be repeated).

If a small *mit-mar-tum* is a feature of the eclipse, the halo....

No. 7. Ritual for Reciting Incantations and Prayers.

This tablet belonged to an Erech ritual, called Lugal ta-è-a. which is also written in Semitic, *Sharru ittaṣâ* "The king goes forth." It furnishes directions for reciting incantations by three classes of priests, as well as for prayers for the king, apparently during a procession through Erech upon the Arammu Kar-azagga, called "the road of the gods," which went as far as the gate of the king, and then to Bît Idkitum. This implies that Erech had a sacred way, which led to, and probably also past, the gate of the king's palace, as at Babylon. Many of the incantations referred to by title are not known.

The tablet was copied from an ancient original in the reign of Antiochus II, in the year, 251 B. C., the same as the text which follows, and for the same individual, Anu-aḫ-ushabshi; but by another son, named, Anu-balatsu-iqbi.

Transliteration.

.......*ša* ^{d}*A-num ištu E-nam-en-na bît pa-pa-ḫa it-ta-ṣa-a*

....*Ka-maḫ KUR-AD* ^{amêl}*mašmašê*^{meš} *gab-bi šipta šarru it-ta-ṣa-a* 3-*šu imannû*(*-nu-u*)

^{amêl}*mašmašê*^{meš} *i-qal-lu-i-ma arki-šu* ^{amêl}*urigallu-u* ^{amêl}*mašmašê*^{meš} ^{amêl}*TU-E*^{meš} *u* ^{amêl}*našê*(*BI-KU*)^{meš} *ša* ^{iṣ}*tal-lu ṣa-an-du*

^{d}*A-num rabû-u šamê*(*-e*) *u irṣitim*(*-tim*) *lik-ru-bu-ka a-na* ^{d}*Anum i-kar-rab*

arku ka-ra-bi ^{amêl}*mašmašê*^{meš} *šipta šarru it-ta-ṣa-a a-di šu-qa ilâni*^{meš} 4-*šu imannû(nu-u)*
^{amêl}*urigallu-ú* ^{amêl}*mašmašê*^{meš} ^{amêl}TU-E^{meš} ^{amêl}*nâšê(BI-KU)*^{meš} *ša* ^{iš}*tal-lu ṣa-an-du*
^{d}*A-num rabu-ú šamê(-e) u irṣitim(-tim) lik-ru-bu-ka a-na* ^{d}*A-num i-kar-rab*

---

arku ka-ra-bi ina su-qa ilâni^{meš} *mašmašê*^{meš} *šipta* l u g a l - e a n - k i - a l u g a l t a - é - a
4-*šu imannû(-nu-ú) šipta i-qal-lu-i-ma* ^{amêl}*urigallu-ú* ^{amêl}*mašmašê*^{meš} ^{amêl}*TU-E*^{meš}
ù na-še-e ^{iš}*tal-lu ki-ma maḫ-ri-im-ma a-na* ^{d}*A-num i-kar-rab*

---

arku ka-ra-bi ^{amêl}*mašmašê*^{meš} *šipta* l u g a l - e e z e n - š i - i n m u - u n - d u
u šipta a - g ù b - b a e l l i t a (- t a) *a-di Kar-azag-ga a-ram-mu ša* ^{giš}*Mà-an-na*
ma-la-ki ilâni^{meš} 7 *TA-A-AN imannû(-nu-ú) šipta i-qal-lu-i-ma* ^{amêl}*urigalli-i*
^{amêl}*mašmašê*^{meš} ^{amêl}*TU-E*^{meš} *na-še-e* ^{iš}*tal-lu a-na* ^{d}*A-num i-kar-rab*

---

ki-ma ša ^{d}*A-num a-na muḫ-ḫi a-ram-mu ša* ^{giš}*Mà-an-na ik-tal-du*
^{amêl}*mašmašê*^{meš} *u* ^{amêl}*TU-E*^{meš} *šipta* g i s - m a - k a s - s i g m u - u n - e l (?) š u - í l - l á - g è
a-na ^{d}*A-num inaššû(ÍL-u) arki-šu* ^{amêl}*urigallu-ú* ^{amêl}*mašmašê*^{meš} ^{amêl}*TU-E*^{meš}
ù na-še-e ^{iš}*tal-lu ka-ra-bi ki-ma maḫ-ri-im-ma ana* ^{d}*Anum i-kar-rab*

---

ištu muḫ-ḫi a-ram-mu e-lu-u ša Kar-azag-ga a-di abulli šarri
^{amêl}*mašmašê*^{meš} *šipta* l u g a l t a - é s i l - a a z a g - g a b a - l u - a - t a 7-*šu imannû(-nu-ú)*
šipta i-qal-lu-i-ma ina abulli šarri ^{amêl}*urigallu-ú* ^{amêl}*mašmašê*^{meš} ^{amêl}*TU-E*^{meš}
ù na-še-e ^{iš}*tal-lu ka-ra-bi ki-ma maḫ-ri-im-ma ana* ^{d}*A-num i-kar-rab*

---

ištu abulli šarri a-di bît id-ki-tum bît ik-kal ^{amêl}*mašmašê*^{meš}

ki-ma ša ina šu-ú-qu ilâni^{meš} *šipâti*^{meš} *imannû(-nu-ú) šipâti*^{me} *i-qal-lu-i-ma.*

^{amêl}*urigalli-i* ^{amêl}*mašmašê*^{meš} ^{amêl}*TU-E*^{meš} *u nâšê(BI-KU) ša* ^{iṣ}*tal-lu*

ṣa-an-du ka-ra-bi adi 7-šu ú-šal-la-mu-ma ana ^{d}*Anum i-kar-rab*

---

ki-ma ša ^{d}*A-num bît id-ki-tum ik-tal-du* ^{amêl}*mašmašê*^{meš}

šipta ê a z a g - g a ê d i n g i r - r i - e - n e *šipta* d i n g i r l u g a l m u - š à d u g - g a - z u - š ù

šipta u n u - k i n - s i g a n - n a - g e *šipta* m e - t e b a r a - m a ḫ *šipta* ú - r i - l i l - ê

u šipta šub-tum ša ilâni^{meš} *rabûti*^{meš} *imannû(-nu-ú)*

---

^{d}*A-num ra-bu-ú šamê(-e) u irṣitim(-tim)* *lik-ru-bu-ka*

^{d}*Ellil* ^{d}*E-a u* ^{d}*Be-lit ilâni*^{meš} *ḫa-diš* *lik-ru-bu-ka*

ilâni^{meš} *ki-lal-la-an* ^{d}*Sin u* ^{d}*Šamaš ina pâni DŪ-ÁM-šu-nu* *lik-ru-bu-ka*

^{d}*Nergal u* ^{d}*Sibi(-bi) ina kun-nu lib-bi-šu-nu* *lik-ru-bu-ka*

^{d}*Igigi ša šamê(-e) u* ^{d}*A-nun-na-ki ša irṣitim(-tim)* *lik-ru-bu-ka*

ilâni^{meš} *ša ap-si-i u ilâni*^{meš} *sa Ku-azag* *lik-ru-bu-ka*

û-mu arḫu u šattu û-mi-šam *lik-ru-bu-ka*

---

an-na-a ka-ra-bi ša ^{amêl}*urigalli-i* ^{amêl}*mašmašê*^{meš} ^{amêl}*TU-E*^{meš}

ù ^{amêl}*nâšê(BI-KU) ša* ^{iṣ}*tal-lu ṣa-an-du iš-tu bît ri-eš*

a-di bît id-ki-tum a-na ^{d}*A-num 7-šu i-kar-rab*

šiptu šarru it-ta-ṣa-a šarru (it-ta-)ittaṣa(E-A)

ki-ma labari-šu šaṭir-ma ba-rum ù ub-ṭu gab-ri ^{iṣ}*pidni ina pani buši* ^{d}*Anu u An-tum*

duppi ^{md}*Anu-aḫ-ušabši(-ši) apil ša* ^{m}*Ki-din-*^{d}*Anu lib-bal-bal* ^{m}*E-kur-za-kir* ^{amêl}*mašmašê*^{meš} ^{d}*Anum u An-tum*

^{amêl}*urigalli-i ša bît ri-eš Uruk*^{ki}*-ú qât* ^{m}*Anu-balaṭ-su-iqbi apil-šu ana a-ḫa-a šimti-šû*

arak ûmê^{meš}*-šu balâṭi napiš-tim u kun-nu išidê*^{meš}*-šu šaṭir-ma ina Uruk*^{ki} *u bît ri-eš*

bît bêl-ú-ti-šu ú-kin pa-liḫ ^{d}*Anu u An-tum ina šuq-qu-nu napišti-šu*

Uruk^{ki} ^{arhu}*Duzu ûmu 25*^{kan} *šattu 61*^{kan} ^{m}*An-ti-'-ku-su šar mâtâti*

ina a-mat ^{d}*Anum u An-tum liš-lim*

. . . . .of Anu, from E-nam-enna, the shrine-house, goes forth,
. . . .*Ka-maḫ* . . .all the magicians, the incantation, **Sharru ittaṣâ** shall recite three times,
the magicians shall burn; and after that, the *urigallû*, the magicians,
the *TU-E* priests, and the bearers of the *tallu* being silent (bound),
"May Anu, the great one of heaven and earth, be gracious unto thee," to Anu, he shall pray.

After the prayer, the magicians shall pronounce the incantation **Sharru ittaṣâ** upon the street of the gods four times.
The *urigallû*, the magicians, the *TU-E* priests, and the bearers of the *tallu*, being silent,
"May Anu, the great one of heaven and earth, be gracious unto thee," to Anu, he shall pray.

After the prayer in the street of the gods, the magicians, the incantation **Lugal-e an-ki-a lugal ta-é-a**
shall recite four times. The incantation they shall burn; and the *urigallû*, the magicians, *TU-E* priests,
and the bearers of the *tallu* (being silent), like the former, he shall pray to Anu.

After the prayer, the magicians, the incantation **Lugal-e ezen-ši-in mu-un-du,**
and the incantation **A-gubba ellita,** upon Kar-azagga, the rampart of *giš-mà-anna*,
the road of the gods, seven times shall recite. The incantation they shall burn, and the *urigallû*,
the magicians, the *TU-E* priests, and the bearers of the *tallu* (being silent) to Anu he shall pray.

As when Anu, upon the rampart of *giš-mà-anna* approaches,
the magicians, and the *TU-E* priests, the incantation **Giš-ma-kas-sig mu-un-el (?) šu-íl-lá-gè,**
to Anu shall lift up. After this the *urigallû*, the magicians, the *TU-E* priests,

and the bearers of the *tallu* (being silent), a prayer like the former, he shall offer to Anu.

From the high rampart of the Kar-azagga, as far as the gate of the king,
the magicians, the incantation, **Lugal-ṭa-ê sil-a azagga ba-lu-a-ta** shall recite seven times.
They shall burn the incantation; and in the gate of the king, the *urigallû*, the magicians, the *TU-E* priests,
and the bearers of the *tallu* (being silent), a prayer, like the former, he shall offer to Anu.

From the gate of the king as far as Bît-Idkitum, the Bît Ikkal, the magicians
the same as in the street of the gods, shall recite incantations; shall burn incantations.
The *urigallû*, the magicians, the *TU-E* priests, and the bearers of the *tallu*
being silent, the prayer, unto seven times, shall render; and to Anu offer.

As when Anu approached Bît Idkitum, the magicians
the incantation **Ê azagga ê dingirrene,** the incantation **Dingir lugal muša dugga-zu-šù,**
the incantation **Unu-kin-sig an-na-ge,** the incantation **Me-te bara-maḫ,** the incantation **Ŭ-ru-lil-ê,**
and the incantation **Šubtum ša ilâni rabûti,** shall recite.

Anu, the great one of heaven and earth, be gracious unto thee.
Ellil, Ea, and the Lady of the gods, joyfully be gracious unto thee.
The gods, both Sin and Shamash, in their fullness, be gracious unto thee.
Nergal and the Sibi, in the firmness of their hearts, be gracious unto thee.
The Igigi of heaven, and the Anunnaki of earth, be gracious unto thee.
The gods of the *apsû*, and the gods of the *Ku-azag*, be gracious unto thee.
Day, month, and year, daily be gracious unto thee.

This is the prayer, when the *urigallû*, the magicians, the *TU-E* priests, and the bearers of the *tallu*, are silent, from Bît Rêsh unto Bît Idkitum, he shall pray to Anu seven times.

"The incantation **Sharru ittaṣâ,**

like its original, is written, collated, and compared. The duplicate of the ritual is in the possession of Anu and Antum.

The tablet of Anu-aḫ-ushabshi, son of Kidin-Anu, the descendant of Ekur-zâkir, the magician of Anu and Antum,

The urigallû of Bît Rêsh, the Erechian, by the hand of Anu-balaṭsu-iqbi, his son, for the sake(?) of his fate,

length of his days, the life of the soul, and to establish his foundations, it is written, and in Erech in the Bît Rêsh,

the house of his lordship, he placed. He reverences Anu and Antum in the ways (?) of his life.

Erech, the month Tammuz, the 25th day, year 61st of Antiochus, king of countries.

By the word of Anu and Antum may it be safe.

No. 8. Bilingual Hymn to the God Anu.

This tablet contains a hymn exalting Anu, the chief god of Erech. It is written in Sumerian with an Akkadian interlinear translation. The colophon informs us that it is the fourth division of a series, known as lugal-e lugal kam-me-ir an-ki-a; and was copied from a tablet in the Library of Anu and Antum at Erech, for Anu-aḫ-ushabshi, a descendant of the well known Erechian family Ekur-zâkir, by his son Anu-ushallim. It is dated in the 61st year of the Seleucid era (i. e. 251 B. C.), in the reign of Antiochus II.

An-na	za-e maḫ-me-en	za-e	maḫ-me-en
ina šamê(-e)	*at-ta ṣi-i-ri*	*at-ta*	*ṣi-ra-at*
ki-i	za-e maḫ-me-en	za-e	maḫ-me-en
ina irṣitim	*at-ta si-i-ri*	*at-ta*	*ṣi-ra-at*
an-na	za-e maḫ-me-en	ki-a	za-e-maḫ-me-en
ina šamê(-e)	*at-ta ṣi-i-ri*	*ina irṣitim(-tim)*	*at-ta ṣi-ra-at*
umun An gal-e	⸗ *be-lu* ^{d}*Anu rabu-ú*	*at-ta ṣi-ra-at*	⸗ za-e maḫ-me-en
umun Unug^{ki}	⸗ *be-lu U-ruk*	*at-ta ṣi-ra-at*	⸗ za-e maḫ-me-en
umun **Ê-ri-eš**		umun Ê-nam-en-na	za-e maḫ-me-en

be-lu *Ê-ri-eš* *be-lu E-nam-en-na* *at-ta ṣ[i-ra-a]t*
umun Ê-šar-ra umun bara-maḫ za-e maḫ-me-en
be-lu *Ê-šar-ra* *be-lu parammaḫu* *at-ta ṣi-ra-at*
umun Ê-éš-gal umun Ê-gal-an-ki-a za-e maḫ-me-en
be-lu E-éš-gal *be-lu ekalli* *šamê(-e) u irṣitim* *at-ta ṣi-ra-at*
umun Ê-an-na umun Ê-ul-maš za-e maḫ-me-en
be-lu *Ê-an-na* *be-lu Ê-ul-maš* *at-ta ṣi-ra-at*
umun E-an-ki-gè umun Ê-giš-sig-an-ki-a za-e maḫ-me-en
be-lu *E-an-ki-gè* *be-lu E-giš-sîg-an-ki-a* *at-ta ṣi-ra-at*
za-e lugal me-en ⸗ *at-ta šar-ri* *at-ta ši-ra-at* ⸗ za-e m[aḫ-me-e]n
. . . . -ma mu-. . . . .
i-dé-íl-la-zu a-ba ba-ra-è *ina*. . . . .
kam-du-zu a-ba ba-ra-šub-bu *ina*. . . . .
á-zid-da-zu ⸗ *ina im-ni-ka aja-bi ul us-ú-ṣu* ⸗ galu erim-manu[è-a]
á-kab-bu-zu ⸗ *ina šu-me-li-ka lim-nu ul i-ba-'* ⸗ ḫul-ma-al nu è-a
si-ig?-giš-ag-a-zu ⸗ *ina giš-pa-ri-ka iṣ-ṣur ul ip-par-ši-du* ⸗ mušen nu ba-šub-ba
šul ka-tar-a-ra-zu íd nu bal-e
ed-lu *mud-dal-lu* *na-a-ri* *ul ib-bir*
me-lám-zu kur-kur-ra ⸗ *me-lam-mu-ka ma-ta-a-ti ka-šu-u* ⸗ sud-sud me-en
ní-gal-zu kur-ra galu erim-ma dul-la-ab
pu-luḫ-ta-ka *ma-a-tu* *aja-bi* *ka-ta-am*

---

e-lum uru-zu *Unug^{ki}-šù* *ud-dam-bi* *ud-du-ma-ra*
kab-tu a-na *a-li-ka U-ruk* *ki-ma ^{d}Šamaš*
rebû(-u) par-su lugal-e lugal kam-me-ir an-ki-a nu al-til
kîma labari-šu šâṭir-ma ba-rum u ub-ṭu gab-ri-e ^{iṣ}pitnu ina pâni buši ^{d}Anu u An-tum
duppu ^{md}Anu-aḫ-ušabši(-ši) mâri ša ^{m}Ki-din-^{d}Anu ^{amêl}lib-bal-bal ^{m}Ekur-za-kir
^{amêl}mašmašu ^{d}Anu u Antum
^{amêl}urigallî ša Bît-ri-eš Uruk^{ki}-u qât ^{md}Anu-ušallim mâri-šu pa-liḫ Anu u An-tum
li-iṣ-ṣur li-ša-qir Uruk^{ki} ^{arḫu}Ululu ûmu 26^{kan} šattu 61^{kan} ^{m}An-ti-'-ku-su šar mâtâti
ina amat ^{d}Anu u An-tum mim-ma ip-pu-uš ina qât-ia liš-lim la-la-a-šu lu-uš-bu

Translation.

1, 2 In heaven, thou lofty one, thou art exalted.
3, 4 In the earth thou lofty one, thou art exalted.
5–6 In the heavens, thou lofty one; in the earth, thou art exalted.
7 Oh great lord, Anu, thou art exalted.
8 Lord of Erech, thou art exalted.

24. *uṣ-u-ṣu* is a scribal error for *us-ṣu-u*.

9–10 Lord of E-rêsh, lord of E-nam-enna, thou art exalted.
11–12 Lord of E-sharra, lord of the sanctuary, thou art exalted.
13–14 Lord of E-esh-gal, lord of E-gal-an-ki-a, the temple of heaven and earth, thou art exalted.
15–16 Lord of E-anna, lord of E-ul-mash, thou art exalted.
17–18 Lord of E-an-ki, lord of E-giš-sig-an-ki-a, thou art exalted.
19 Thou art king, thou art exalted.
20–21 . . . .
22 When thou raiseth thy countenance, who does not go forth?
23 When thou withdraweth thyself, who does not prostrate himself?
24 From thy right hand, the enemy will not escape.
25 From thy left side, the evil doer will not slip away.
26 From thy snare, the bird will not fly away.
27–28 [Thy] worshipping hero will not cross the river.
29 Thy glory overspreads the lands.
30–31 Thy fear covers the land of the enemy.

32–33 "Honored one, for thy city Erech, it glows like the sun."
34 Fourth section of **Lugal-e lugal kammer an-ki-ia** It is incomplete.
35 Like its original, is written, reviewed, and collated. The copy of the document is among the treasures of Anu and Antum.
36 Tablet of Anu-aḫ-ushabshi, son of Kidin-Anu, descendant Ekur-zâkir, the magician of Anu and Antum,
37 the *urigallû* of Bît Rêsh, the Erechian; by the hand of Anu-ushallim, his son, the worshipper of Anu and Antum,
38 which may he protect, may he regard precious. Erech, 26th of Elul, 61st year of Antiochus, king of lands.
39 By the command of Anu and Antum, whatever I do by my hand, may it be acceptable; may I be satisfied with its elegance.

No. 9. A Bilingual Babylonian Lamentation.

Some of the lines that have been preserved of this bilingual (Sumero-Akkadian) inscription, which is from a lamentation ritual, strikingly recall the opening lines of the Book of Lamentations. If Jerusalem, which is pictured as a mother, is substituted for "the mother goddess," the lines are almost identical. Besides the overthrown home and city, the lines referring to the defiled abode, the plundered possession, as well as the desolation, misery, and departed glory of the city, curiously remind of the Jewish dirge. While the picture is not as elaborately drawn, the misery and pathos is as complete as in Lamentations. The destruction of the city, indirectly caused by the invader, is heightened by the natural conditions of the country. The penitential character of the Biblical Lamentations is wanting, at least in this tablet; which, it should be added, however, is doubtless only one of a series, and may represent only a portion of the complete dirge.

The tablet is unbaked. The script and the tablets with which it was found suggest that it was written in the Greek period at Erech. The mistakes, omissions and failure to recognize signs in the original, from which this version or copy was made, besides other evidences, clearly show that the scribe was either a learner, or he was deficient in his understanding of the language of the text.

Transliteration.

ás mu-lu al-di-di *e-diš-ši-šu i-dal e-diš-ši-šu i-dal* áš mu-lu al-di-di
ama mu-gig-ib na-àm urú-na-šù ⁝ *um-ma iš-ta-rit áš-šum âli-šu*
gašan ê-a na-àm gil-[sa-]a-na-šù ⁝ *be-lit bîti áš-šum šú-kut-ti-šu*
na-àm urú-ni gul-a-ni ⁝ *áš-šum âḷi-ša ša i'-ab-ti*
na-àm E-an-na ḫul-a-ni ⁝ *áš-šum bi-tim-ši ša uš-pi(?)-líl*
na-àm MAL+DU-na pä-el-lá-na ⁝ *áš-šum maš-ta-ki-šu ša ul-te-'-ú*
na-àm urú-ba sí(g)-ga-na ⁝ *Xáš-šum ri-šit-ti-šu ša is-sa-pan*
na-àm mu-un-ga àg-kar-kar-ra-bi ⁝ *áš-šum ma-ak-kur-ša ša im-šu-ša-'*
na-àm gíl-sa-ab a til-la-mu ⁝ *áš-šum šu-kut-ti-ša ša ig-gam-mar*
erim šú-gul uku ḫub-bi-eš-a-na ⁝ *i-šit-ta-šu it-ta-bat ni-šú-šu it-tak-mar*

10. The character sa apparently is omitted, cf. line 16.

12. The text reads *ta-mar-líl*, but perhaps the scribe should have written *ušaplil* or *uš-pi-el;* cf. also li. 22.

13. The scribe apparently wrote ama wrongly, instead of the sign MAL+DU = *maštaku*, cf. *B*. 5488. Note pi-el-la = *la'u;* cf. pi-el-la *B*. 7977.

14. The root of *rišittu* is *rašâdu*.

15. The character *ša* in *um-šu-ša-'* seems to be superfluous. For kar-kar = *maša'u*, cf. *SAI* 5729.

17. Here šú-gul = *abâtu*, cf. šú-gul-la = *maḫâṣu*, DISGl p. 109, and gul = *abâtu*, li. 11 above. Ḫub-bi-eš = *ik-mur*, cf. *BA* V, 533:25, and *SAI* 1767. Since ḫub-bi-eš here also is singular perhaps eš is part of the ideogram.

urú azag-ga lîl-lá-áš sìg-ge-da : *âlu el-lu ana za-qi-qi it-tur*
urú engur-ra a mu-da-an-dé : *a-lum ša ki-ma ap-par mu-u ub-lu-šu*
engur-ra ki šub-ba a mu-da-an-dé : *ap-par a-šar na-di-i mu-u ub-lu-šu*
mu-gi da-ma-al izi mu-da-an-šub : *ana a-pi rap-šu i-ša-a-tu it-ta-an-di*
ê azag-ga šú-ḫul ab-ba(or um-ma)-KA : *bîti el-lu uš-pi-lil*
^{im}šu-rin-na-eš-ám a-dìm ba-an-da-ri-ri : *a-ši-bu-šu ki-i* [*me*] *it-taš-lal*
[GU] ku-ni-eš-ám engur-dìm ba-an-da-dé : *nap-ḫar a*[*-ši*]*-bu-šu* [*ki-i*]
ṣi-rim im-ta-lu-u
[ki-b]i ir-ra-bi nu-un-zu : *a-šar iš-šal-lum ul i-di*
[ki-bi ir-ra-]bi nu-un-má-má-bi : *a-šar iš-šal-lum a-ba-ru ul a-li-e*
[kaskal ir-ra-bi] nu-un-z-u : *ḫar-ra-nu iš-šal-lum ul i-di*
[kaskal ir-ra-bi] nu-un-má-má-bi : *ḫar-ra-nu iš-šal-lum a-ba-ru ul a-li-e*
. . . . ra-é : . . . *-ru-šua -šar ip-par-šu·it-ta-ṣa*(*ša*)
. . . . su . . . .
. . . . dub nu-te-en-te-en
[mu-gig-ib na-àm uru]-na E-an-na ù-nu-ku-ku : *iš-ta-rit áš-šum âli-ša*
áš-šum bîti-ša ul i-ṣal-lal
[aš-ám] mu-lu nu-kúš-ù : *e-diš-ši-šu uš-tan-na-ḫa KI-MIN*
[nun-na aš-ám mu-lu] nu-kúš-ù : *ru-bat e-diš-ši-šu uš-tan-na-ḫa*
[azag Nin]-líl aš mu-lu nu-kúš-ù : *el-lit ^{d}Ištar e-diš-ši-šu uš-tan-na-ḫa*
[. . . . .] dúb ki ba-pa-nu : *ilu KIMIN* hi-bi-eš-šu
[nu-al]-di-di me-ri-a-ni i-ní-si
ù-nu-ku i-dè-ni ni-ma-al
nu-kúš-ù á-na ni-ma-al
ê-a ê-a im-tu-tu : *bîtâti^{meš} i-te-nir-ru-bu*

18. sig-gi-da=*ittur.*

19. Engur=*apparu.* Like sug, it has this value as well as *apsû.*

21. Here mu-gi=*ana a-pi*, cf. gis-gi=^{giš}*abu*, B. 2386. *Ki* is apparently a mistake of the scribe for *di.*

23. Ri-ri=*šalâlu*, cf. ri=*šalâlu*, *B.* 2576. It seems *me-e* is omitted in the Akkadian.

24. In the Akkadian *ši* and *ki-i* seem to have been omitted by the scribe.

26. Cf. má-má=*bašû* B. 5430, etc. It would seem that the scribe changed *a-ma-ru* in lines 26 and 28 into *a-ba-ru;* cf. note on li. 44.

29. The scribe made the last character *ša*; but *ṣa* seems to be necessary.

33. Here nu-kúš-u=*anâḫu;* but cf. *la a-ni-ḫa* B. 2000.

e-sil e-sír-ra gú-mu-un-sír-sír : *su-qa ana su-qa ul-ta-nar-ru*
saḫar sil-damal-la . i-dè : *i-pi-ru ri-ba-a-tu aš-uš-ba-rit*
i-de-zu-bar ír-ra sa ba-nád : *i-na pî-ša ki-niš ip-pa-la-su da-me im-ta-la-'*
mu-lu dam ḫul nu mu-un-da pád-mu : *ša itti mu-ut ḫa-du-ú a-ba(ma)-ru*
ul a-li-e
mu-lu dumu ḫúl nu-mu-un-da pád-mu
mu-lu bi ê tùr-ra nu : *ú-tul-la-šu ina tar-ba-za KIMIN KIMIN*
síb-bi amaš-a-ni nu : *ri-e-um-šu ina su-bur KIMIN KIMIN ba*
dam-da ná-a-ra i-dè mu-un-(?) : *ša* (*ana*) *itti mu-ut ṣal-lum tap-*
pa-at ḫi bi-eš-šu
dumu-da ná-a-ra i-dè-gâ-gâ : *ša it-ti ma-ri* (*ṣal*)*-lu ta-bar-ri*
dam-da ná-a-ra i-lu mu-un-na-ab : *ša it-ti mu-ut ṣal-lum qu-ba-a i-qab-bi*
dumu-da ná-a-ra i-lu mu-un-na-ab : *ša it-ti ma-ri ṣal-lum qu-ba i-gab-bi*
ê-sag ki-ku-ba mi-ni-íb-dar-dar : *eš-rit-šu-nu ina šub-ti-šu-nu-tu ut-ri-ir*
erim-ma kaskal-a-šù mu-un-ma-al : *i-sit-tim ana ḫar-ra-nu taš-kun*
áš-âm mu-lu me-li-[e-a] áš-âm mu-lu me-li-[e]-a

41. E-sil=*sûqu*, is new.

41. sir-sir=*šeru*, *šurru* (*CT* XIX, 21:17f) gú-tug=*šarû B.* 3314 (II *R* 29:5c), gú-lal=*šarru* B. 3306. Here gu-sir-sir apparently=*šerû*. Note that *ul-ta-nar-ru* is an example of II^{III}.

42. It would seem *uš* is a mistake for *ta*. Even so the form *aš-ta-ba-rit* appears to be a conundrum..

43. Cf. i-de-bar-ra-zu=*tappalasi* (*B.* 4010). Here nád apparently=*malû*.

44. In personal names da=*lê'u* "to be able" cf. Tallqvist *Neub. Namen.*, and Clay *PN*. It would seem that *a-ba-ru* was originally *a-ma-ru*; cf. pád=*âtû* (B. 9412) and *amâru* (B. 9411); see also lines 26 and 28; in fact the scribe seems to have altered his writing, being uncertain of his reading.

47. The scribe mistook the sign *su* for *qâtu*, and wrote that character.

48. The Babylonian text was injured (*ḫibeššu*); and the scribe apparently could not read the verbal element in the Sumerian, for he has made something which is indistinct, and which is by no means intelligible.

49. The scribe omitted *ṣal* in the Akkadian. Igi . . . gă=*barû* cf. DlSGl p. 20.

50. I-lu mu-un-na-ab-bi also I-lu mu-na-bi=*qubâ iqabbi* cf. DlSGr p. 115. This is construed as having the infix nab, since bi=*qabû* and *nabû*, *B.* 5124. Apparently ab also=*qabû*, cf. *BA* V 678:23 and perhaps also 711:10. It is to be noted that na as well as nab is an infix with dative signification (see DlSGr 166). Unless the scribe in lines 50 and 51 omitted the verbal element bi, it would seem that the verbal element is ab and in the passage quoted above ab-bi. Cf. also ^{d}ab-ba =^{d}*Nabû*.

52. Cf. dar=*tarru*, *B.* 3494. Since the prt. I of *tarâru* is *itrur*, the form must be *utarrir*=*utârir*=*utrir*.

e-diš-ši-šu i-nim-[ma] e-diš-ši-šu i-nim-ma
me-li-e-a ni-[gub ᴬ *i-nim-ma az-za-zu*
me-li-e-a ni-[tuš ᴬ *i-nim-ma uš-ša-ab*
me-li-e-a ni [šàg-sur ᴬ *i-nim-ma a-na-ḫum*
me-li-e-a ni-tu ᴬ *i-nim-ma ir-ru-bu*
me-li-e-a ni-te-en-te-en ᴬ *i-nim-ma a-[pa-aš-ša-ḫu]*
. . . . ᴬ *na . . . . . . ni-šu*

Translation.

She goes about lonely; she goes about lonely,
The mother-goddess, because of that city,
The mistress of that house, because of its furnishings;
Because of that city, which was destroyed;
Because of her house, which was overthrown;
Because of its abode, which was defiled;
Because of its establishment, which was overthrown;
Because of its possession, which was plundered;
Because of its furnishing, which was ruined;
Its festival was ruined; its people was exterminated.
The holy city became like a ruin heap.
The city, the water brought it like unto a marsh.
(Like unto a) swamp, a place of ruin, the water brought it.
Like a wide reed, into the fire it was thrown.
The holy house was laid low.
Its population, like [water], is carried away.
All its inhabitants became like a waste.
The place it was carried, I do not know.
The place it was carried, I am unable to cross over to.
The road it was carried, I do not know.
The road it was carried, I am unable to cross over to.
Its . . . . . . the place it flew, it went forth.
. . . .
. . . .
The goddess because of her city, because of her house, will not lie down to sleep.
She alone will lament.
The princess alone laments.

The holy Ishtar alone laments.
The god.......*injured* (i. e. the original)
She went not on her journey, she was full of awe.
She did not lie down; she lifted her eyes.
She did not rest; she exerted her strength.
The houses they entered.
They wandered from street to street.
The dust of the square they....
On her word truly they looked; they became covered with blood.
The one with a joyful husband, I am unable to see.
The one with a joyful child, I am unable to see.
Its herd in the stable, (I am unable to see).
Its shepherd in the fold, (I am unable to see).
Who, with husband sleeping, the companion..*injured* (i. e. the original)
Who, with child sleeping, is filled with woe.
Who, with husband sleeping, she cries aloud wailing.
Who, with child sleeping, she cries aloud wailing.
Their shrines in those dwellings, are wrecked.
The meal on the road, she placed.
Alone is she now.
Now I will stand.
Now I will dwell.
Now I will lament.
Now I will enter.
Now I am satisfied.

No. 10. Bilingual Hymn to Ishtar.

This is an edition of the well known hymn, written in honor of Ishtar, versions of which were found in the Library of Ashurbanipal (668–626 B. C.), and in the Temple Library at Babylon, belonging to the Greek period.[1] The present text was very probably found at Erech, and may also have been written in the Greek era.

[1] See Delitzsch *Ass. Les.*[3] 135 ff, and Reisner *Sumerisch-Babylonische Hymnen* No. 53 For the transliteration and translation of the text see Banks *Sumerisch-Babylonische Hymnen* (Dissertation); Hussey *AJSL* 23, 156 ff; and Jensen *KB* VI 2 120; and for translation only, see Langdon *Sumerian and Babylonian Psalms* 180 ff.

It is a part of the sixth tablet of the series U r u ḫ u l - a - g e (*ša âli ša šulputu*) "He of the city of destruction cries." The importance of the present text lies in its variants.

No. 11. A Lamentation Addressed to the Word of Enlil.

This is also a copy of a well known lamentation.[1] It was designated U d - d a m k i - á m - u š (*ša kîma ûmu suršudu*) "which like the day (or spirit) is founded." It offers variations which will be important for the future study of the poem. It is dated in the 108th year of the Seleucid era in the reign of Antiochus III.

No. 12. Divination by Hepatoscopy.

This text is almost perfectly preserved. Like other baked tablets from Erech belonging to the Greek period, the clay is very light in appearance. It is dated in the 98th year of the Seleucid era, in the reign of Antiochus III. It is the sixth tablet of the *ubânu* (i. e. omens concerning the *ubânu*, the finger shaped appendix of the liver, called *processus pyramidalis*), and it is the fifty-fifth tablet of the *bârûtu* series (i. e. omens of the inspection series). The colophon adds: "it is not complete", meaning it is not the final tablet of this class of the omen series. It begins: "If on the surface to the right of the *ubânu*, a finger is marked; the prince shall seize booty".

No. 13. Divination by Means of the Viscera.

This tablet is quite similar in appearance to the former; and it is nearly as well preserved. It is dated a year later, and belonged to the same priest, Nidintum-Anu, who was probably connected with the temple Eanna, at Erech. It is the third tablet of the *šummu tirâni* (i. e. omens beginning with these words), and the seventh tablet of the *bârûtu* series. The transliteration of this tablet is given below, in which the viscera, probably of the abdomen, are likened to different objects, some of which are as yet unknown.

The special interest of this text lies in the historical references which are contained in it. Line 33, reads: "If the *tirâni* is like an eagle; it is the omen of Etana the king who ascended to heaven." In the

[1] See Reisner *Sumerisch-Babylonische Hymnen* 1-3; Banks *ibid.*, etc.

dynastic list recently published,[1] Etana, who lived in the fifth millennium B. C., is called "a shepherd." The forecast, which was probably well understood by the priest, is not mentioned. It is hoped that another omen text will be found that will furnish this.

Line 18 contains "the omen of Narâm-Sin, who overthrew Apirak in arms." This summarizes one of the two well known omens of that great ruler. The other known omen refers to the conquest of Magan.[2] In lines 34, 35, and 55, the forecast simply reads: "omen of Narâm-Sin." It is probable that they were understood to refer to the forecast already mentioned in line 18.

Line 65 contains an omen which is very important for the reconstruction of the early history of Amurru. It reads: "If the *tirâni* is like the face of ^{d}*Ḫum-Ḫum*; an usurper of the land will rule the world." A fragment of a text in the British Museum published by Boissier, reproduces the first part of six lines of this text (i. e. 63 to 68),[3] the third of which reads: "If the *tirâni* is like the face of *Ḫum-ba-ba*," etc. This shows that the ideogram ^{d}*Ḫum-Ḫum* is to be read Ḫumbaba.[4]

As the writer has shown, Ḫumbaba, the despot with whom Gilgamesh fought, did not live in Elam nor was he an Elamite god, but a human being who lived in the Lebanon region.[5] Following is a transliteration and translation of this text.

TRANSLITERATION.

Šumma tirânu kîma

Š. t. k. *ki-pi pit(-it) pal-e mâti iṣaḫḫir lu-ub-nu ina mâti ibašši(-ši) ú-lu šarru ina umanni(-ni) ittiṣi-ma itti umanni (-ni)-šu inakir(-ir)*

š. t. k. *azkaru umanni(-ni) rubî mâḫira la iši(-ši)*

š. t. k. *pit-pa-nu DAG-GAB piristu(-tu) šarru ḫammû*

š. t. k. *gam-lim kišittum(-tum)*

š. t. k. ^{iṣ}*qaštu ana imni rubû illatê*^{meš}*-šu ibbalkatû*^{meš}*-šu-ma u-šam-qat-šu*

[1] Poebel *Historical Texts* p. 73.

[2] See King *Chronicles* I, p. 33 ff.

[3] Boissier *Choix de Texts Relatifs à la Divination*, p. 91.

[4] ^{d}*Ḫum-Ḫum* occurs in names of the Neo-Babylonian period, cf. ^{d}*Ḫum-Ḫum-ab-uṣur*, etc. See Tallqvist, *Namenbuch*, p. 249; also see *SAI* 8580.

[5] Clay *Empire of the Amorites* 87 f; and *A Hebrew Deluge Story in Cuneiform*, p. 49 f.

š. t. k. *^{iṣ}qaštu ana šumêli nakru illatê^{meš}-šu ibbalkatu^{meš}-šu-ma u-šam-qat-šu*

š. t. k. *irâti^{meš} šir eli qurâdê^{meš}(-e)-šu pu-u-tu imaqut(-ut)*

š. t. k. *rîmu rubû nakrê^{meš}-šu eqâm(-qam)*

š. t. k. *rêmu rêmu ina mâti i-dan-nin*

š. t. k. *gam-lim-ma eliš Šu-Nigin-Ḫa innamrû^{meš} kišittum(-tum)*

š. t. k. *gam-lim-ma šapliš Šu-Nigin-Ḫa innamrû^{meš} tîbu*

š. t. k. *el-lam Ku-Ši palî rubî inakir(-ir) ṭêmu mâti išanni(-ni)*

š. t. k. *el-lam Pu-Ḫi-Dir a-ku ina birki amêli ibašši(-si)*

š. t. k. *ši-kin libbi aḫê^{meš} rubî ina âli-šu iṭ-ṭar-rad-ma ina mâti šarrûtim(-tim)-ma itarriṣ(-iṣ)*

š. t. k. *libbi nûni šarru i-dan-nin-ma mâḫira la iši(-ši)*

š. t. k. *ir-ri šipâti^{meš} piristu(-tu) Na-ram-^{d}Sin ša A-pi-rak ina gam-lim isaḫḫap*

š. t. k. *nikis(-is) rîmi-ma eli minâti^{meš}-šu ik-bi-ru ḫušaḫḫi še'i tibni u šamni ina mâti rubî ibašši(-ši)*

š. t. k. *qû^{meš} šipâti^{meš} niṣirta bâbâni^{meš} u-paḫ-ḫir*

š. t. k. *qar-qu-ru nabalkatu(-tu) kap-pi šuḫluqti mât Akkadu^{ki}*

š. t. k. *i-ši-'-ti ^{iṣ}erši ^{d}En-lil ana mâti ana limitti u-šar-ri*

š. t. k. *i-ši-'-ti ^{iṣ}kussî mâtâti^{meš} innakirû^{meš}-ma kussû(Aš-Te) kussâ (Aš-Te) i-tar-ri-is*

š. t. k. *ṣal-lim ša ^{amêl}addubi saḫ-maš-tum u marṣu ina mâti ibašši(-ši)*

š. t. k. *pikurtu pat-lu piristu(-tu) marṣu ana mâti rubî itbam(-am)*

š. t. k. *ṣiru it-gu-ru tibû ana šarri bartum*

š. t. k. *Pap šubti-ka a-na šubti nakri-ka iššir(-ir)*

š. t. k. *kakkabu umanni(-ni) rubî mâḫira la iši(-ši)*

š. t. k. *ḫallu ṭêm mâti išanni(-ni)*

š. t. k. *maš-ti ili u ^{il}Ištar marṣu eli ummanni(-ni)-ia unaddi(-di)*

š. t. k. *gišimmaru ba-ru-ú ina libbi ummanni(-ni)-ia illikû^{meš}*

š. t. k. *našru piristu(-tu) ^{il}E-ta-na šarru ša ana šamê(-e) itêlu(-u)*

š. t. k. *pa-aš-tu piristu(-tu) ^{m}Na-ram-^{d}Sin*

š. t. k. *a-ri-tu piristu(-tu) ^{m}Na-ram-^{d}Sin*

š. t. k. *ka-ba-bu šarru i-dan-nin-ma mâḫira la iši(-ši)*

š. t. k. *lîtu tanittu(Zag-Sal) ṣab rubî ina kabti-šu imaqut(**-ut**)*

š. t. k. *^{iṣ}nalbantu ^{amêl}nakru mât rubî ana qi-rib ittur(-ur)*

š. t. k. *šu-kut-tim ṣi-e rubû alâni^{meš}-šu ana Im-Tab-Tab-ba innakurû^{meš}-šu*

š. t. k. *^{abnu}i-ba-ri rubû šubat-su ana qi-rib etêrub(-ub)*

ṣ. t. k. ^{abnu}*pulukku* ^{amêl}*nakru šubat-su ana qi-rib etêrub(-ub)*
š. t. k. ^{abnu}*pulukku šanû*^{meš} *enšûti*^{meš} ^{iṣ}*kakku šarri kênu*
š. t. k. ^{iṣ}*ribḫu kup-pu-tu rubû šubta u-za-qar-ru ú. . . .*
š. t. k. ^{iṣ}*ribḫu kup-pu-tu-ma šanû*^{meš} *ensûti*^{meš} *libbi bêli mâti la Si-(?)*
š. t. k. e-gi-i ^{iṣ}*kakki šarri kênu*
š. t. k. maṣḫatu zaq-ru lalû^{meš}*-šu lalû*^{meš}*-šu-nu imallû*^{meš}
š. t. k. kubšu kussu(Aš-Te) kussâ(Aš-Te) i-tar-ri-iṣ
š. t. k. qaqqadi aggulli ṣab rubî mâḫira la iši(-ši)
š. t. k. pu-qut-ti nabalkutu(-tu) kap-pi
š. t. k. ḫar-ḫar-ri te-šu-u
š. t. k. ḫal-ḫal-la-tu pî-ia ana ummanni(-ni) imaqut(-ut)
š. t. k. tim-bu-ut-ti manzaz ^{d}*Ištar-ia libbi umanni-ia itti ilâni*^{meš} *Kar(-mi)*
š. t. k. li-li-si ana pî išten(-en) mâtu uššab(-ab)
š. t. k. ṣi-ṣi-i-tum par-ga-niš u a-bur-reš uššab(-ab)
š. t. k. paṭru ana riksi piristu(-tu) ^{m}*Na-ram-*^{d}*Sin*
š. t. k. pâšu [u] paṭru ilu ikkal
š. t. k. naglabi^{amêl} *gallabi šarru qarradê*^{meš} *iši(-ši)*
š. t. k. šanû-ma ana maḫrûti^{meš}*-šu-nu illikû*^{meš} *ana arkâti*^{meš}*-šu-nu na-aḫ-su mâḫiru nap-ša mâti ikkal*
š. t. k. šanû-ma ana arkâti^{meš}*-šu-nu illikû*^{meš} *ana maḫrûti*^{meš}*-šu-nu na-aḫ-su biblu mâti ub-bal*
š. t. k. Nag-Miš ^{iṣ}*kakki šarri kênu*
š. t. k. Ne-Za-Za ^{d}*En-lil ana mâti ana limutti u-šar-ra tâmtu ub-bal* ^{d}*Adad iraḫiṣ(-iṣ) zunnû*^{meš} *iḫappû*^{meš} *âlu šubâti*^{meš} *šubâti*^{meš} *im-mu-u-nu-ma ekalli i-ḫar-ru-ub*
š. t. k. zîmi alpi ummanni(-ni) rubî mâḫira la iši(-ši)
š. t. k. kal-bi ummani(-ni) rubî mâḫira la iši(-ši)
š. t. k. pâni Ḫumbaba(^{d}*Ḫum-Ḫum) piristu(-tu) ḫammû ša mâti kalama i-be-el*
š. t. k. aqrabi ekalli iraššî-ma ^{iṣ}*kakki šarri kênu*
š. t. k. Lam-Kid-Maḫ šar kiš-ša-ti ina mâti ibašši(-sî)
š. t. k. Gud-Elim ku-sa-ri-iq ša-nu mat-su kussa(Aš-Te) uššab(-ab)
š. t. k. Gud-Gud-Ná ma-ḫi-ṣi rîm(-im)-ma ana imni itariṣû^{meš} *dan-an šarri u ummani(-ni)-šu*
ṣâb šarri iqabbû-ma illikû(-ku) mâḫira la iši(-ši)

š. t. k. Gud-Gud-Na ma-ḫi-ṣi rîm(-im)-ma ana šumêli itariṣû^{meš}
dan-an nakri u ummani(-ni)-šu
ṣâb nakri iqabbû-ma illikû(-ku) mâḫira la iši(-ši)

š. t. k. šu-uš-kal-li piristu(-tu) a-kal-šu lu ša ^{amêl}*ša-tam* ^{amêl}*Uš*^{meš}
ša ina libbi ummani(-ni)-šu
ana SHID(?) ul nâri imtaqut(-ut)

75 *š. t. k. qaqqadi pilaqqi ṭêm mâti išanni*

š. t. k. rit-ti amêltûi ḫušaḫḫu ina mâti ibašši(-ši)

š. t. k. šepi amêlûti ḫarran ^{d}*I-šum*

duppu 3^{kan}*-ma šummu tirâni duppu 7*^{kan}*-ma ku-kar ba-ru-tu nu al-til*
šumma ekalli tirâni la ušabši(-ši) palî šarri uqatti kussû(Aš-Te) inakir(-ir) bêlu ul-la uš-an-ni

duppu ^{m}*Nidintum-*^{d}*Anu apil ša* ^{m}*Anu-bêl-šu-nu apil* ^{m}*E-kur-za-kir* ^{h}*mašmaši* ^{d}*Anu u An-tu qât* ^{m}*Anu-aḫ-ušabši(-ši) apil-sa*
apil ša ^{m}*Ina-qi-bit-*^{d}*Anu apil* ^{m}*E-kur-za-kir* ^{h}*masmasu* ^{d}*Anu u An-tum Uruk*^{ki} ^{arḫu}*Airu ûmu 7*^{kan} 139^{ka} ^{m}*An-ti-'-ku-su šarru*
ina a-mat ^{d}*Anu u An-tum liš-lim*

Translation.

If the *tirâni* are like

" an open arch(?); the reign of the land will be short; there will be a disaster in the land,
or the king will abandon his army; and with his army there will be a change.

" a moon-crescent; the army of the prince will not have a rival.

" a long broken stretched out(?)-bow; the omen of an usurper.

5 " a *gamlu* weapon; conquest.

" a bow on the right; the prince's forces will rebel against him and overthrow him.

" a bow on the left; the enemy's forces will rebel against him, and overthrow him.

" breasts; a serpent will fall upon his vanguard.

" a bull; the prince will resist his enemies.

10 " a vulva; mercy will be strong in the land.

" a *gamlu* weapon, and above is seen a fishnet; conquest.

" a *gamlu* weapon, and below is seen a fishnet; an attack.

" *el-lam Ku-Ši;* the reign of the prince will change; conditions of the land will be altered.

If the *tirâni* are like

" *el-lam Pu-Ḫi-Dir;* there will be weakness in the penis of the man.

" the shape of a heart; the brothers of the prince will be driven from the city, and sovereignty in the land will be extended.

" the heart of a fish; the king will be strong and he will not have a rival.

" a rope of wool; the omen of Narâm-Sin who overthrew Apirak in arms.

" a decapitated bull, and extended beyond its size; there will be a famine of grain,

straw and vegetables in the land of the prince.

" woolen threads; he shall gather the treasure of the gates.

" a *qarquru*; rebellion of a wing (of the army); destruction of the land of Akkad.

" the outline of a bed; Enlil will wander over the land for evil.

" the outline of a throne; the lands will be estranged, and dynasty will oppose dynasty.

" the apron of the *addubu;* there will be rebellion and sickness in the land.

" a twisted cord; the omen is, sickness will come to the land.

" a wriggling serpent; an attack on the king; a revolt.

" *Pap;* thy capital will succeed against the capital of thy enemy.

" a star; the army of the prince will not have a rival.

" a *hallu;* the spirit of the land will change.

" a drinking jar of the god and goddess; disease will fall upon my army.

" a date palm; contentment will go from the heart of the army.

" an eagle; the omen of Etana, the king, who went up to heaven.

" a two-edged sword; the omen of Narâm-Sin.

" a shield; the omen of Narâm-Sin.

" a flame; the king will be strong, and will not have a rival.

" a *tanittu* cow; the soldier of the prince will fall in his conceit.

" a brick-mould; the enemy will return to the land of the prince for a conflict.

" a *šukuttim*; the prince's cities will be estranged from him on account of duplicity.

" an *ibaru* stone; the prince will enter his capital for a conflict.

" a *pulukku* stone; the enemy will enter his capital for a conflict.

If the *tirâni* are like

" a thin-double *pulukku;* the weapon of the king is true.

" a *kupputu ribḫu;* the prince will elevate his capital, and...

" a *kupputu ribḫu* and it is thin-double; the heart of the land's lord will not...

" a fence(?); the weapon of the king is true.

" a pointed *maṣḫatu;* his luxuriousness (and) their luxuriousness will be full.

" a cap; dynasty will oppose dynasty.

" the head of a pike; the soldier of the prince will not have a rival.

" a thorn-bush; rebellion of a wing (of the army).

" a *ḫarḫarri;* revolution.

" a timbrel; my word to the army will fail.

" a seal-ring with the place (?) for my goddess; the heart of my army with the gods will...

" a *lilisi;* according to one mouth, the land will dwell.

" a *ṣiṣîtum;* the (land) will dwell in security and in safety.

" a dagger on a belt; the omen of Narâm-Sin.

" an ax and a dagger; the deity will consume.

" the razor of a barber; the king will possess warriors.

" double, and they went to their faces, to their backs they recede; price will consume the abundance of the land.

" double and they went to their backs, to their faces they recede; the produce of the land will increase.

" *Nag-Miš;* the weapon of the king is true.

" *Ne-Za-Za*; Enlil will wander about the land for evil, the sea will swell, Adad inundate, rains will devastate, city buildings and dwellings will be ruined, and the palace will be destroyed.

" the face of an ox; the army of the prince will not have a rival.

" a dog; the army of the prince will not have a rival.

" the face of Ḫumbaba; the omen is, a usurper of a land will rule the world.

" a scorpion; the temple will be rich; the weapon of the king will be true.

" *Lam-Kid-Maḫ;* a king of hosts will be in the land.

" a *kusariqqu;* a second of his land will sit on the throne.

" *Gud-Gud-Na*, fighting bull, and extends to the right; the forces of the king and his army will say:

'a soldier of the king' and they shall march; he will not have a rival.

If the *tirâni* are like

" *Gud-Gud-Ná*, fighting bulls(?), and extends to the left; the forces of the enemy and his army shall say:

'soldier of the enemy,' and march; he will not have a rival.

" a net; the omen is his food...of the *shatammu*, the *Uš* who in his army for a........will not fall(?)

" the head of an ax; the intelligence of the land will change.

" a human hand; there will be a famine in the land.

" a human foot; it is the affair of the god Ishum

Tablet 3 of *šummu tirâni;* tablet 7 of the *bârûtu* series. It is not complete.

If there is not a temple of the intestines; the reign of the king will end; the dynasty will change; a remote master will return.

Tablet of Nidintum-Anu, son of Anu-bêlshunu, family of Ekur-zâkir, the magician of Anu and Antu; by the hand of Anu-aḫ-ushabshi,

son of Ina-qibit-Anu, son of Ekur-zâkir, the magician of Anu and Antum. Erech, month Airu, day 7th, year 139th of Antiochus.

Nos. 15 and 16. Divination by Means of the Viscera.

These two texts, apparently written by Assyrian scribes, were copies of Babylonian originals. Only the reverse of each tablet has been preserved. They duplicate the contents of each other, and furnish some important variations. The transliteration given below is based on both texts. The one tablet was written by Ili-ma-aḫu, the seer, and the other by Ṭâb-ṣili-...

Transliteration.

Šumma ina ekalli ti-ra-ni

š. i. e. t. zi-ma eli ti-ra-ni ir-kab rubû mâti.... ....

š. i. e. t. zi-ma eli imni ti-ra-ni ir-kab rubû...........

š. i. e. t. zi-ma eli šumêli ti-ra-ni ir-kab rubû ša mâti.......

š. i. e. t. na-si-iḫ-ma eli imni ti-ra-ni ir-kab rubû mâti........

š. i. e. t. na-si-iḫ-ma eli šumêli ti-ra-ni ir-kab $^{am\hat{e}l}$nakru mâti rubî-šu...

š. i. e. t. na-si-iḫ-ma ana arkat(-at) ti-ra-ni imakut(-ut) šarru i-da-an-ni-in-ma mâḫira la ibašši

š. i. e. t. zi-iḫ-...-ma $^{\check{s}ir}$birku atru ekalli rubî iṣ-ṣa-ap-pa-'

š. i. e. t. [di]-ig-š[u] iz-zi-iz ti-bu-um

š. i. e. t. $^{\check{s}ir}$[irru] atru it-tab-ši rubâ ina ekalli-šu i-ba-ar-ru-uš

š. i. e. t. $^{\check{s}ir}$irru at-ru pa-ri-ik rubâ ina ekalli-šu idâkû$^{me\check{s}}$-šu

š. i. e. t. $^{\check{s}ir}$irru at-ru [um]-ma-[tu] ib-ni mâr tuq-ma-at-ti $^{i\check{s}}$kuṣṣa iṣabat(-at)

š. i. e. t. par-rum ina imni iššakin(-in) [ekalli] rubî $^{am\hat{e}l}$nakra i-liq-qi

š. i. e. t. par-rum ina šumêli iššakin(-in) [ekalli] $^{am\hat{e}l}$nakri rubâ i-liq-qi

š. i. e. t. ti-bu qi-ta-nu [ti-ra-ni] iššakin(-in) rubû ia-a-bi-šu qât-zu i-kaš-šid

š. i. e. t. $^{i\check{s}}$kakku a-ri-du uṣ[ṣi-ma el]i ti-ra-ni irkab-ma šur-ru-ur ù imkut(-ut) ardi šarri.......

š. i. e. t. $^{i\check{s}}$kakku a-ri-du uṣṣi-ma eli imni ti-ra-ni ir-kab a-kal nam-ra

3. The duplicate text (see line 1), has *nakru* instead of *rubû*.

7. The other text, li. 5, uses the ideogram *SA*. It is unfortunate that *zi-iḫ-* is not complete.

7. The variant text has *sigišše*, which may have been repeated. This ideogram has the value *balû* "to go to ruin, be destroyed," *naqû* "to pour out," etc. Dúb, which means *ṣibû*, also means *šapâku, tabâku sarâqu* (S^c 35 ff.) "to pour out;" cf. *ṣāpāteka*. Ezek. 32: 6. Cf. the palace shall be dissolved (*namôg*), Nahum 2:7.

8. Cf. *K*. 8272:3, Boissier *Choix de Textes Relatifs à la Divination* p. 87.

9. Cf. *ibid.* li. 4.

11. For *tuq-ma-at-ti* the variant text reads *BE.MU.SU*. That this is probably an ideogram for *tuqumtu* appears reasonable when it is considered that *BE* has such values as *laqâtu, naqâru, šagâmu*, etc.

14. Cf. *zi-bu* K. 8272:5 Boissier *ibidem*, p. 87. On *zi-bu* = *tibû*, see Jastrow *Religion* II 780, note 2.

15. Cf. *DUL-GUB*, Boissier, *ibid.* p. 87, li. 6, and B. 9596.

16. On *namâru* cf. Jastrow *Religion* II 103.

š. i. e. t. ^{iṣ}*kakku a-ri-du uššì-ma* [*eli*] *šumêli ti-ra-ni ir-kab zinništu eṭirtum*(*-tum*)

Summa ekallu ti-ra-ni

š. e. t. šina(*-na*) *marê*[^{meš} *šarri*] ^{iṣ}*kuṣṣi a-bi-šu i-ṣa-bat*

š. e. t. šina-ma šak-nit-tum eli a[*-ḫu*]*-u ir-kab rubû šarrut*(*-ut*) *kiš-šu-ti i-ṣa-bat*

š. e. t. šina-ma a-ḫi-tum eli rêšan êlati(*-ti*) *irkab rubû ana* [^{amêl}*nakri-šu*] *kalû išakan*(*-an*)

š. e. t. šalaštu marê^{meš} *šarri ana* ^{iṣ}*kuṣṣi a-bi-šu-nu ana limutti*(*-ti*) *i-te-ib-bu-ú*

š. e. t. šalaštu-ma ištenit(*-it*) *ina imni ištenit*(*-it*) [*ina*] *šumêli* [*šaknat*] *be-el-tum* ^{iṣ}*kuṣṣa i-ṣa-bat*

š. e. t. šalaštu-ma ištenit(*-it*) [*a-ri-ik*] *ištenit*(*-it*) *ik-ru* ^{iṣ}*kuṣṣu i-na-ak-ki-ir*

š. e. t. šinâ-ma im-nu-ú šarrâni(*lugal-e-ne*) *in-ni-im-mi-du-ma mâta ibêlû*^{meš} (*-lu*)

š. e. t. šinâ-ma šu-me-lu-ú šarrâni(*lugal-e-ne*) *in-ni-im-mi-du-ma mâta la ibêlû*^{meš}(*-lu*)

š. e. t. šinâ-ma ina imni iššakanû^{meš}(*-nu*) *ši-bu-tu in-ni-im-mi-du-ma mâta i-bi-lu*

š. e. t. šinâ-ma ina šumêli iššakanû^{meš}(*-nu*) *KIMIN-ma mâta la i-be-el-lu*

š. e. t. na-si-iḫ-ma ina imni ti-ra-ni um-ma-ta ib-ni rubû ina âli-šu iṭ-ṭa-rad-ma
ina mâti išanni-ma it-ta-nam-giš

š. e. t. na-si-iḫ-ma ina šumêli ti-ra-ni um-ma-ta ib-ni rubû ša mâti ^{amêl}*mihra*

š. e. t. ti[*-ra-ni*] *ana šinâ*(*-na*) *i-zu-uz te-im mâti* (*i-*)*išanni*(*-ni*) *napḫar išten šu-ši šumma ti-ra-ni qât* ^{m}*I-li-ma-aḫ*. . .

18. The duplicate text, li. 16, reads "sons of the king shall strive (*iš-ta-an-na-an-nu*) for the throne of their father."

21. Instead of *limutti*(*-ti*) *i-te-ib-bu-u*, the duplicate text reads *SA.SA-nu*, which is to be read *ištannannu*(*-nu*), cf. *SA*=*šanânu* B. 9539, and Jastrow *Religion* II 848. *Šanânu* in II[1] has the meaning "to rival, combat, fight." Cf. also *SA.SA*=*dâlu* "to slander," *dabâbu* "to calumniate," etc.

Translation.

If in the temple of the intestines

" a face pass over the intestines; the prince of the land.....

" a face pass over the right of the intestines; the prince......

" a face pass over the left of the intestines; the prince of the land...

" there is a separation, and it pass over the right of the intestines; the prince shall [seize] the land [of the enemy]

" there is a separation, and it pass over the left of the intestines; the enemy will [seize] the land of the prince.

" there is a separation, and it falls to the rear; the king shall be strong, and will not have a rival.

" is *zi-ih*...., and there is a superfluous shoot; the palace of the prince shall be dissolved.

" a split exist; an uprising.

" there is a superfluous intestine; the prince they shall see in his palace.

" a superfluous intestine is separated; the prince they shall kill in his palace.

" a superfluous intestine form a mass; a son of strife shall seize the throne.

" a break(?) is on the right; the palace of the prince shall take the enemy.

" a break(?) is on the left; the palace of the enemy shall take the prince.

" a club is at the end (?) of the intestine; the prince shall capture his enemy by his hand.

" a hanging weapon come out, and pass over the right of the intestine and is brilliant, and fall; the servant of the king...

" a hanging weapon come out and ride over the right of the intestine; food is possessed.

" a hanging weapon come out and ride over the left of the intestine; a woman is the deliverer.

If the temple of the intestines is double; a son of the king shall seize the throne of his father.

If the temple of the intestines is double, and a *šaknittum* ride over the side; the prince shall seize a powerful kingdom.

If the temple of the intestines
" is double, and the side ride over the top of the head; the prince shall establish a hold upon his enemy.
" is triple; sons of the king shall advance with evil intent against the throne of their father.
" is triple, and one is on the right, one is on the left; a lady shall seize the throne.
" is triple, and one is long, one is short; the dynasty shall change.
" is double, and they are right; kings shall be established, and they shall rule the land.
" is double, and they are left, kings shall be established, and they will not rule the land.
" is double, and they are on the right; elders shall be established, and they shall rule the land.
" is double, and they are on the left; elders shall be established, and they shall not rule the land.
" is separated and a mass is formed on the right; the prince shall be driven from his city, and
there shall be a change in the land, and it shall be overthrown.
" is separated, and is formed a mass on the left; the prince of the land shall have a rival.
" divide into two; the spirit of the land shall be changed.
Total 60 *šumma tirâni*, by the hand of Ili-ma-aḫu, [the seer].

No. 17. Sumerian Incantation for an Evil Tongue.

This Sumerian text partially duplicates the ninth tablet of the Shurpu Series,[1] a copy of which belonged to the Library of Ashurbanipal. The present inscription enables us to make some corrections in the text that has been restored from a number of fragments in the British Museum; which text, on the other hand, enables us to complete several lines that have been injured in the present text. In the duplicate ê "house" is written a "water," and ú "vegetable" is written û "day." Apparently the Assyrian scribe wrote the tablet from a dictation.

[1] See Zimmern *Shurpu* (*AB* 12), 44 ff.

En ^{giš}šinig ^{giš}dil dingir edin-na
pa-zu an-šù úr-zu ki-šù
pa-zu an-šù giš bur-bur-ra
úr-zu ki-šù te-me-en sĭg-ga
šab-bi-zu dingir-ri-e-ne
pa-bi sag-bi sag ê tŭ-ám
ka lù-gàl-lu mu-un-el-la mu-un-láḫ-láḫ-ga
ka(eme) ḫul-gál bar-šù ḫe-im-ta-gub

En úin-nu-uš ú el abzu-ta sar-a
an-šù pa-zu ki-šù úr sag
an-šù pa-zu ki-šù ne-in-tág
ki-šù úr-zu ki-šù mu-un-el
šab-bi pa-zu šakan ḫe-ši-in-láḫ-láḫ-ga
pa-bi sag-ba sag-ba ê tŭ-ám
ka l-ùgàl-lu mu-un-el-la mu-un-láḫ-láḫ-ga
eme ḫul-gál bar-šù ḫe-im-ta-gub

En gi-azag gi-el gi-šàg-ga sar-a
an-ta ba-mul ki-ta ba-mul
an-ta ki-ta mul-mul ne-[ib-si]
an-ta šú-si-di ki ^{d}[Babbar-ge]
ki-ta šú-luḫ šú-dŭ ^{d}En-k[i-ga-ge]
sag-ge ê tŭ-am giš-bur-bur-[ra]
lùgàl-lu sag-ge ê tŭ-ám ka-bi a-ra-an-bi
ka lù-gàl-lu mu-un-el-la
eme ḫul bar-šù ḫe-im-ta-gub

---

1. Cf. ^{u}dil, Küchler *Med* p. 32.

4. The variant reconstructed text reads sîg-ga "green" foundation. See Zimmern *Surpu* IX.

7. The sign âlu is apparently intended for gàl.

8. The first sign is apparently intended for eme; cf. the variant text *Surpu* p. XVII.

14. Also 22, 23, and 31. The word ê (*bîtu*) is written instead of a (*mê*); cf. *Surpu* XVII 14, 20, 21 and 29.

18-22 are restored from the variant text; see *Surpu* LXXIII.

22-23. Note the scribe's variations in the writing of ge and ê.

25. Apparently gâl was omitted by the scribe.

En elteg-si ka lug-ga azag-azag-ga
ᵘukuš sag gar-si-si sĭg-ga
eš-bar ka-azag nam-ta-ri
eme te-bi im-mi-in-(?)-dûb-bu
eme te-bi im-mi-in-te-en-te-en
lù-gàl-lu- sag-ga ê tŭ-âm ka-bi a-ra-an-bi
ka lù-gàl-lu mu-un-el-lu mu-un-láḫ-láḫ-ga
eme ḫul-gál bar-šù ḫe-im-ta-gub

Incantation: O tamarisk, the divine *dil* tree of the plain!
Thy branch (is) in the heaven, thy root (is) in the earth.
Thy branch (is) in the heaven, O tree of redemption.
Thy root (is) in the earth, O foundation of grace.
Thy twig (is) of the gods
Its branch (is) the ban, the ban of the libation house.
The mouth of the man becomes clean, becomes pure.
Let the evil tongue stand aside.

Incantation: O *mashtakal*, thou holy plant, grown in the sea,
In the heaven (is) thy branch, in the earth is the root of the ban.
In the heaven (is) thy branch, to the earth it is thrown down.
In the earth (is) thy root, in the earth it is pure.
The twig of the branch, may it purify the bowl.
Its branch is the ban, the ban of the libation house.
The mouth of the man becomes clean, becomes pure.
Let the evil tongue stand aside.

Incantation: O pure reed, holy reed, grown in the *gi-sag-ga*;
Above it shines, below it shines.
Above (and) below it is filled with splendor.
Above is the hand of justice, the hand of Shamash.
Below is the performing rite of Ea.
O ban of the libation house, O tree of redemption,

26. Elteg-si=*uḫulu qarnânu;* see Küchler *Med.* p. 106.

27. The variant text instead of ú, reads û; which it would seem was a mistake see *Surpu* XVII:25. On [ú] gar-si-si cf. *M.* 9288.

29. The variant reads dub-dub-ba; cf. *Surpu* XVII:27.

O man, the ban of the libation house, has pronounced its word for thee.
The mouth of the man becomes pure.
Let the evil tongue stand aside.

Incantation: O *elteg-si*, cleanse (and) purify the mouth.
O cucumber the ban, gracious *gar-si-si*,
Decide the fate of the pure mouth.
The language of its propitiation appeases him.
The language of its propitiation reconciles him.
O man, the ban of the libation house has pronounced its word for thee.
The mouth of the man becomes clean,. becomes pure.
Let the evil tongue stand aside.

Nos. 18 to 35. Miscellaneous Texts.

No. 18 is an incantation for an evil spell caused by a witch. Texts Nos. 19 and 20 bear upon astrology; the latter, entitled "the star and thy register for the tenth of Nisan," explains the formulæ for horoscopic forecasts. Nos. 21 to 24 are omens. No. 25 is a calendar specifying the days of the months Marchesvan, Kislev, and Tebet, when certain rites were performed in temples throughout Babylonia. The identification of some of the gods with certain temples and cities, is important. These are included in the Index of Names. Nos. 26 to 28 are lists of occupations, names, etc.; these, with the syllabaries and explanatory texts, Nos. 29 to 35, will be included in the lists which are being prepared for publication, by Dr. Ettalene M. Grice, of the Yale Babylonian Seminary. No. 35 was previously published by Père Scheil, in *Recueil de Travaux*, 27, p. 125.

No. 36. Multiplication Table 160,000 × 1.

This tablet contains the multiplication table 160,000 × 1 on the obverse, and 24 × 1 on the reverse. In the former table, the number is written five times thus 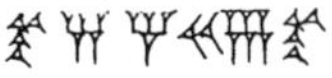. This would equal 9,736,000. Either  should be omitted, or it has a significance which has not been recognized. If this is omitted, the number is 160,000, and all the calculations hold out, even the square of it in lines 24 and 25, namely 160,000 × 160,000 = 25,600,000,000.

This number 160,000 is a divisor of 12,960,000; but not all multiplication tables are, as has been heretofore assumed, for in the Yale Collection there is an 800,000 × 1 table. In the closing lines of both tables the number is squared; and then the total is said to be the square of it. The reverse reads: 24 a-ra 24 576 576-e 24 ám ib-di; i. e., "24 × 24 = 576; 576 is the square of 24." The tablet is dated mu [d]En-lîl gìr-ra, an unidentified date, apparently of the Ḫammurabi era.

No. 37. Divisions of the Shar-Gal.

This tablet contains the divisors and quotients of 12,960,000, or 60 raised to the fourth power, the number so extensively used in early Babylonian mathematical texts; and which in Sumerian was called Shar-Gal. Plato regarded it as the number of the days of the earth's lifetime, which he called the "geometrical number" (γεωμετρικός). Several fragments of similar texts have been published, for which the list of the divisors and quotients has been restored.[1] The present text, however, is complete. The opening lines read:

1 (i. e., 12,960,000)	⅔-bi(i. e., its two-thirds	=) 8,640,000 ám
šú-ri-a-	bi(i. e., its half	=) 6,480,000
igi-3-gal-	bi(i. e., its third	=) 4,320,000 etc.

As heretofore observed only the divisors of this number, namely ⅔, ½, ⅓, etc., with their quotients, are given, up to $\frac{1}{64}$; but the next divisor in the texts is not 72, but it is 81. Even the published text upon which the supposed 72 is based, is to be read 81.[2] The present text, as well as *YBC* 7303, shows this. Why the divisors 72 and 80 are omitted in all these texts is not clear. The last divisor given in all of them is 81.

Nos. 38–42. Mathematical Texts.

No. 38 is a 10 × 1 multiplication table, dated in the 28th year of Samsu-iluna; No. 39 is a 16×1 table. Nos. 40 and 41 are metrological tables; and No. 42 gives the squares of numbers from 20 upwards.

[1] See Hilprecht *BE* XX, 20, 21, 22, and 25; and Pinches *H A V*, p. 72.
[2] See *BE* XX 20 Rev. Col. IV, 28.

No. 43. Bronze Canephorous Statue of Ur-Engur.

This bronze statue was first presented in a little monograph entitled *Ur-Engur, a Bronze of the Fourth Millennium in the Library of J. Pierpont Morgan*, by C. H. W. Johns, Litt.D. It is not only the oldest of such statues, but it is the largest and finest known. It stands 33 cm. high. The inscription reads: "Ur-Engur, king of Ur, king of Sumer and Akkad, who built the temple of Enlil." Ur-Engur, we now know, ruled at Ur from about 2474 to 2456 B. C. The Collection also possesses the stone tablet bearing the same inscription, such as have usually been found with these statues. They were discovered at Nippur. Nothing has been found at that site to compare with the statue as a work of art.

No. 44. Votive Tablet of Ur-Engur.

The inscription of this stone votive tablet reads: "To Innina the mistress of Eanna, his goddess, Ur-Engur the mighty hero, king of Ur, king of Sumer, and Akkad, her temple he built and restored."

No. 45. Onyx Bowl Dedicated on the Birth of a Prince.

The greenish onyx bowl containing this inscription was found at Warka. It was dedicated to the god on the occasion of a prince being born to Lugal Kisalsi, apparently the King of Erech, who ruled about 3100 B. C. The inscription reads: "To the god Urra, by the priest Abu-ḫadu, for a son of Lugal Kisalsi, born of his wife Muḫarsagni, has been presented."[1]

No. 46. Fragment of a Jar Dedicated to the Goddess Nisaba.

This inscription is on a part of the rim of a large pottery jar, which measured about fifteen inches in diameter. The dedicatory inscription of the jar reads: "to Nisaba, the loyal lady, the gracious lady, the magnificent lady, the beloved of the god Anu, the lustrous one of the lands, the lady with sevenfold intelligence (?), seven hands (?), fourteen[2] intelligent (?) ears, exalted scribe of Anu, the . . . . of Enlil, ...

[1] See Banks *Amer. Jour. of Sem. Lang.* XXI 62f.

[2] It was published by Scheil *OLZ* VII, 254 f., since which time it has suffered considerably from disintegration, and instead of "eighteen" it seems to appear to read "fourteen."

No. 47. Inscribed Votive Object of Kurigalzu.

In the dark center of the agate cameo, the following inscription appears: ᵈEn-lil lugal-a-ni-ir Ku-ri-gal-zu a-mu-ru "To Enlil, his lord, Kurigalzu has presented." Kurigalzu lived about 1300 B. C. It probably was found at Nippur at the time excavations were conducted at that site. Fragments of two other specimens of the same ruler were found, and are now preserved in the Ottoman Museum, in Constantinople.[1]

No. 48. Inscribed Votive Object of Nebuchadnezzar II.

Encircling the dark center of an agate cameo there is engraved the following inscription of Nebuchadnezzar (604–561 B. C.): *Ana ᵈMarduk bêli-šu ᵈNabû-kudurri-uṣur šar Bâbiliᵏⁱ mâr ᵈNabû-apal-uṣur ana balâṭi-šu iqîš* "To Marduk, his lord, Nebuchadnezzar, king of Babylon, son of Nabopolassar, presented for his life."

The object presumably was found at Babylon, the patron god of which city was Marduk. This idea is supported by the fact that a similar one, though smaller, and not so symmetrical, was found by the expedition under Koldewey in the ruins of that city.[2]

No. 49. Annals of Arik-dên-ilu.

This fragment contains the earliest annals from Assyria at present known, and the only historical record of the Assyrian king Arik-dên-ilu, who ruled about 1300 B. C. Besides it, there are known a short dedicatory inscription on a limestone cylinder,[3] and an inscribed brick[4] of this king. The present fragment, which is a part of a large tablet, may prove of great value when other fragments of the same text are found.[5]

No. 50. A Charter of Sin-shum-lîshir.

The deed or charter which is represented by this fragment has been regarded as having been granted by Sin-shar-ishkun, one of the last

[1] See Hilprecht *OBI*, Nos. 134 and 135.
[2] See Koldewey *Die Tempel von Babylon und Borsippa*, Abb. 76.
[3] See King *Annals of Assyrian Kings* I, p3.
[4] See Lenormant *Choir de Textes Cuneiformes* No. 72 169f.
[5] The text is here published for the first time; the transliteration was published by Scheil *OLZ*, VII 216f.

kings of Assyria.[1] On this fragment has been based the claim that Sin-shar-ishkun was a son of Ashurbanipal, and a brother of Ashur-etil-ilâni, who succeeded Ashurbanipal; but the traces preserved of the second and third elements of the name point rather to another ruler, whose name is known at present only from the date of a single contract tablet which is in the Metropolitan Museum, namely Sin-shum-lîshir[2] king of Assyria. It has been assumed that the brief reign[3] of this ruler, Sin-shum-lîshir, followed that of Ashur-etil-ilâni, because the name of the only other known ruler, before the fall of Nineveh, that of Sin-shar-ishkun, is identified with the Greek Sarakos, whom Abydenus tells us was the last king of Assyria.

According to the improved reading of the name in the text, as here offered, namely Sin-shum-lîshir, the son of Ashurbanipal, the necessity disappears for regarding the ruler fourth removed from that great king as his son. The importance of this fragment is confined to these facts, since little more of the document is preserved than enough to determine its general character.

No. 51. Building Inscription of Nabopolassar.

The inscription refers to the building operations of Nabopolassar (625–604 B. C.) at Babylon. It was baked too long, which resulted in the cylinder losing its symmetrical shape, and in the injury of some of the text. It is written in the monumental script, as are other inscriptions of this ruler. The transliteration and translation follow:

^{d}*Na-bi-um-apal-*[*u-ṣu-ur*]	Nabopolassar,
šarru dannu [*šar Bâbili*^{ki}]	the mighty king,
šar ^{ma}[^{t}*Su-me-eri-im u Ak-ka-di-i*^{ki}]	king of Sumer and Akkad,
ša [*pa-la-aḫ Ilu u Ištar*]	who reverences Ilu and Ishtar
ru[*bam na-'-dam ti-r*]*i-iṣ ga-at*	the exalted prince, directed by the hand of
^{d}*Na-bi-um i* [^{d}*Marduk*] *a-na-ku*	Nabû and Marduk, am I.
ni-nu-um il[*i*(*NI-NI*) *r*]*a-be-u-tim*	When the great gods

[1] The name has thus been read by Scheil, who published the text and translation, *ZA* XI, 47 ff. With the exception of a few minor points besides the reading of the name here discussed the text does not differ from that previously published.

[2] Clay, *B. E.*, VIII, 141.

[3] The Tablet is dated on the 13th day of the accession year. Unfortunately the month is not given.

a-na be-lu-ut ma-a-ti šu-ma-am ṣi-ri-im	pronounced the lofty name for the
ib-bu-u ḫa-aṭ-ṭa pi-ri-ik-ti	lordship of the land, entrusted to me a despotic sceptre
a-na ri-te-id-di-e ni-ši-ia	to govern my people,
i-qi-pu-u-ni ^{is}*uš-pa-ri-im ṣi-ri-im*	and placed in my hands the exalted reins[1]
[a-]na ku-nu-uš la ma-gi-ri-im	for the subjugation of
u-ša-at-mi-iḫ ga-tu-u-a	of the refractory,
in û-mi-šu-ma na-ap-ḫa-ar um-ma-ni-ia	In that day, upon all my workmen
tu-up-ši-ik-ku lu e-mi-id	I placed the *tupšikku*.
^{is}*al-lu* ^{is}*ma-ri-im lu u-ša-aš-ši-im*	The hoe and spade I caused to be borne by
ni-ší ma-a-ti e-li-ti ù ša-ap-li-tim	the people of the upper and nether land,
ša ^{d}*Na-bi-um ù* ^{d}*Marduk ṣi-ri-ši-na*	with which forces Nebo and Marduk
a-na ga-ti-ia ú-ma-al-lu-ú	filled my hand.
^{d}*Ur-ra be-li-.........li-....*	Urra, the lord of.....
im-ni-ia ra-bi...........sa	on my right.......
II ....*be-a*	....
............*ki*..........	....
............*um-ma*................	....
......^{d}*Marduk ra-be-a*........	....Marduk the great
......*a-na im-tab-ba*.........	.......to
ni-ni û-mi-šu ni-mit-ti-[^{d}*Bel]*	When in that day, Nimitti-Bêl
e-iš-ši-iš lu ab-ni-ma a-na ^{d}*Marduk be-lí-ia*	Verily I built anew; and for Marduk, my lord,
ki-ma û-mi-im lu-u-na-mi-ir	verily I made shine like the day.
ma-aṣ-ṣa-ar-ti E-sag-ila u Bâb-ili^{meš}	The guarding of Esagila and Babylon
lu u-da-ni-in mârê^{meš} *Ba-bi-lam*^{ki}	truly I strengthened. The sons of Babylon
šu-ub-ti ne-eḫ-ti lu u-še-ši-ib	in a restful dwelling place, truly I made dwell.

[1] Cf. Jensen *K B*, VI p. 440.

Ba-bi-lam^{ki} *ma-ḫa-aṣ bêli ra-be-im* ^{d}*Marduk*	Babylon, the city of the great lord Marduk,
ki-ma ša û-mu-um u-ul-lu-tim	as in former times,
a-na ta-na-da-a-ti lu aš-ta-ka-an	for magnificence, verily I established.
^{d}*Marduk* ^{d}*En-lil ili*(*NI-NI*) *a-ši-ir ki-ib-ra-a-tim*	May Marduk, the Enlil of the gods, the director of the quarters,
e-ib-ši-ti-ia da-am-ga-a-tim	upon my pious deeds
ḫa-di-iš na-ap-li-is-ma ḫa-aṭ-ṭa	joyfully look; and a righteous
i-ša-ar-tim ^{iṣ}*kakku qalû šu-ur-šu-da*	sceptre, improved arms, an established
pa-li-e û-mu-um ri-e-qu-tim	reign for the future,
in ki-ib-ra-tim ar-ba-'-im	in the four quarters,
in ri-ša šamê(*-e*) *LAL-A-tim ši-ta-ad-du-*	exalted in the full joy of heaven,
in qi-be-ti-ka ṣi-ir[*tim*]	by thy lofty command,
[*a-na*] *ši-ri-iq-tim šar-ru-tu*[*-ia*]	[as] a gift to [my] kingship,
[*šu-ur-qi-im*]	[present]

No. 52. Marriage Contract from Mesopotamia.

Owing to the fact that excavations have not been conducted in the middle Mesopotamian region, only five cuneiform inscriptions that have been published have come from that district. The exact provenance of the present document, one of the five,[1] which teems with interest and important data, is not known; yet it is safe to say that it was found in the land, called in ancient times Ḫana, the home of the gods Dagan, Shamash, and Itur-Mer, near the river Ḫabur. It was written in the reign of Ḫammu-rabi'.[2] Whether this ruler is to be identified with the great law-giver of the First dynasty of Babylon, or with another bearing that name, who lived perhaps in the Cassite period, cannot definitely be determined. The seal impression, however, as

[1] See Clay *Empire of the Amorites* 111 ff, on the other four inscriptions.

[2] On the reading *Ḫammu-rabi'* instead of *Ḫammu-rabiḫ* (*-rawi*, *-rawiḫ* or *-rafi*) see Clay *Empire of the Amorites*, 113 ff. In spite of the fact that Albright considers it now "absolutely certain" that Luckenbill's 'Ammurawiḫ, and the meaning of the name "the clan is wide" are correct (*Jour. Pal. Or. Soc.* I : 70), it would seem that he will need to furnish a little more data besides finding that a form of that root, not in a personal name, was used in So. Arabic. If *Reḫab-'am* means "he has extended the tribe," does *Reḫab-Jahu* mean "he has extended Jahu"? In the Cassite period and that of the First Dynasty the *aḫ*, *iḫ*, sign is frequently used for the breathing.

far as known to the writer, is peculiar to the Cassite period. The fact that the name of the Çassite god Bugash is found on the tablet, in the name of the canal Ḫabur-ibal-Bugash, seems also to point to the time of Cassite influence.

The text which has been published and translated[1] is here republished with some modifications. It should be noted that the names of the two cities in the date formula, which have been read and frequently reproduced, as *Zakku-Isharlim* and *Zakku Igitlim*, should be read *Dûr Isharlim* and *Dûr Igitlim*.

ᵐKi-ik-ki-nu mâr ᵐA-ba-ia	Kikkinu, the son of Abaia,
i-na bu-ul-ti-šú ši-im-ti ša ᶠBi-ti-ᵈDa-gan	by his generosity, the lot of Bitti-Dagan,
aššati-šú i-ši-mu	his wife, determined:
ᵐKi-ik-ki-nu mût-za	Kikkinu is her husband;
ᶠBi-it-ti-ᵈDa-gan aššat-zu	Bitti-Dagan is his wife.
šum-ma ᵐKi-ik-ki-nu mût-za	If Kikkinu, her husband,
a-na ᶠBi-it-ti-ᵈDa-gan aššati-šú	to Bitti-Dagan, his wife,
ú-ul aššati-mi at-ti i-qa-ab-bi	shall say: 'thou art not my wife,'
ri-qu-zu i-na bîti-šú ú-ṣi	empty handed she shall leave his house;
a-na alpê^meš ekalli u-tar-ḫu-šu	with the oxen of the palace he shall herd her.
ù šum-ma ᶠBi-it-ti-ᵈDa-gan aššat-zu	And if Bitti-Dagan, his wife
a-na Ki-ik-ki-nu mûti-ša	to Kikkinu, her husband,
ú-ul mûti-mi at-ta i-qa-ab-bi	shall say: 'thou art not my husband,'
e-ri-ši-ša ú-ṣi a-na bît ru-uk-ba-at	she shall leave her bed; to the carriage house of the
ekalli ú-še-il-lu-ši	palace, he shall cause her to go.
marê^meš ᶠBi-it-ti-ᵈDa-gan	The children of Bitti-Dagan,

[1] See Johns *PSBA* 1907, 177 ff.

2 Probably *bultišu* is to be identified with the Hebrew בֹּשֶׁת.

5 *Bitti-Dagan* probably means "Daughter (בת) of Dagan."

10 The word *u-tar-ḫu-šu* is Amorite from the root ארח to wander, go, cf. Job 34 : 8. Cf. also אֲרֻחָה "meal, food:" see *A Hebrew Deluge Story*, p. 62.

14 *Erišti* seems to be an Amorite word from the same root as *eršu* "bed," cf. עֶרֶשׂ "marriage couch," Cant. 1 : 16.

ša a-na Ki-ik-ki-nu mûti-ša ú-ul-[lid]	which to Kikkinu, her husband, she bore,
zitti i-na bîti ^{m}Ki-ik-ki-ni [mûti-ša]	a share in the house of Kikkinu, [her husband]
i-ka-lu ^{m}Ki-ik-k[i-nu mûti-ša]	shall enjoy. Kikkinu, [her husband]
^{m}Apil-^{d}Adad. . . .	Apil-Adad. . . . .
a-na ^{f}Bi-it-[ti-^{d}Da-gan]. . . .	to Bitti-Dagan. . . . . .
a-na ma-ri ik.	to. . . . .
(two lines erased)	
. . . .	. . . .
ša-da-.	. . . .
da-ba- [bi.	complaint. . . . .
nîš ili ù [šarri it-mu]	By the god and [the king they swore].
mahar Pa-gi-rum	Before Pagirum.
^{arhu}Bi-ri-iṣ-ṣa-ar-ru ûmu 17^{kan}	The month Biriṣṣarru, day 17th,
šattu ^{m}Ḫa-am-mu-ra-bi-' šarru*	the year when Ḫammurabi', the king,
^{nâr}Ḫa-bur-i-ba-al-Bu-ga-aš	dug the canal Ḫabur-ibal-Bugash
iš-tu ^{al}Dûr I-šar-li-im	from the city Dûr-Isharlim
a-na ^{al}Dûr I-gi-it-li-im	to the city
ip-tu-ú	Dûr-Igitlim,

No. 53. List of Cities.

The importance of this inscription is in the large number of towns named in it. It belonged to the temple administrative archives of a temple, probably of Lagash. The text was previously published in the conventional Assyrian character.[1] It is here presented with some modifications, and in the script of the tablet. The cities are listed in the Index of Names.

Nos. 54 to 57. Bullae of the Greek Period.

Several thousands of more or less round clay objects, containing seal impressions, but uninscribed, have been found by the Arabs at Warka. The seal impressions on them indicate that they all belong to the Greek period. Every one of the several thousand seen by the

[1] See Scheil *RT*, 20, 68 ff.

writer is baked. They can be said to belong to the class of objects which have been termed "bullae"; and correspond to the many that have been found, although of a different shape, belonging to other periods, especially the Ur dynasty.

Most of these bullae are literally covered with seal impressions. The smallest contains two or three, while the largest contains many. One reproduced on Plate VI contains no less than forty impressions, every one of which is different. Unquestionably this means that forty different individuals are represented on the object by the impressions of their seals, which are equivalent to their signatures. On some of the larger bullae there is an irregular line composed of little circles running between the seal impressions (see Plate VI). In one instance there are ten of these little circles composing the line, which were apparently made by a minute tube, perhaps a small reed. This line doubtless was made to show where the impressions begin and end; for on the one side of it the impressions are more scattered than on the other, indicating apparently where they begin; while on the other side of the line, where they end, the impressions are considerably crowded together.

These bullae appear to have been used like those, published and discussed by Dr. Keiser, in Part III, of this series, belonging to the Ur Dynasty, two thousand years earlier. They were lumps of clay which had been pressed upon a light cord, encircling some reed like object; and in some instances a heavier cord or rope. After they had served their purpose as bullae, they were baked and preserved as a record. The large bulla with forty impressions, described above, has a round hole 3.15 centimetres in diameter.

The motifs of many of these seal impressions are Babylonian and Persian; yet some found among them are Grecian. Of special interest are several of the latter here presented which bear Greek inscriptions. (See also Plate VI.)

No. 54. The centre of this seal contains an emblem or design. The inscription reads ΑΛΙΚΗ ΟΡΧΩΝ "The salt-works of Erech". This reading and interpretation seems reasonable because of the fact that business transactions in salt frequently occur in the contracts and letters from Erech.[1]

[1] See Clay *Neo-Babylonian Letters from Erech.* I am indebted to my colleague, Professor Torrey, for assistance in deciphering the faintly preserved Greek words.

No. 55. This seal contains a standing figure leaning upon a stand and touching what is probably an altar with a wand or spit. The inscription reads ΧΡΕΟΦΥΛΑΚ[ΟΣ] ΟΡΧΩΝ "The public accountant of Erech".[1]

No. 56. The impression of this seal is very indistinct. It has also a standing figure with an inscription of a similar character; but the office is different. It reads [?]ΧΟ[?]ΦΥΛΑΚ[OS] ΟΡΧΩ[N]

No. 57. This seal contains a well executed head, encircled with a garland. It is inscribed on the left side, ΕΝ ΟΡΧΟΙΣ "in Erech." The right side of the impression is incomplete; it doubtless contained the office. The head is probably of one of the Seleucid kings.

No. 58. Greek Inscription on a Jar-Cover.

The exact provenance of this terra-cotta jar-cover is not known; but presumably it was found at Erech. The inscription reads: ΑΡΙΣΤΕΑΣ ΩΙ ΑΛΛΟ ΟΝΟΜΑ ΑΡΔΙΒΗΛΤΕΙΟΣ "Aristeas, whose other name was Ardi-Bêlti." In Part II of the present series, several persons were quoted as having assumed a second name; for example, we find, *Nanâ-iddina ša šumišu šanû ᵈDimetiria* "Nanâ-iddin whose other name was Demetrios." It seems in this period the custom of changing even one Babylonian name to another was also practised.[2]

[1] Speleers has published a similar inscription which he reads Χρεοφύλλακκος(sic) Ωρχῶν "du comptable public des Orchoéniens." *Catalogue des Intailles et Empreintes Orientales des Musées Royaux du Cinquantenaire*, p. 234.

[2] See Clay *BRM* II p. 16.

NAME INDICES

NAME INDICES

Abbreviations

anc.	ancestor	f.	father
b.	brother	gf.	grandfather
BRM.	Babylonian Records in the Library of Mr. J. Pierpont Morgan	hus.	husband
		MLC.	Morgan Library Collection
		s.	son
d.	daughter	wi.	wife

Personal Names

Names of Gods

Names of Places

Names of Temples

AUTOGRAPHED TEXTS

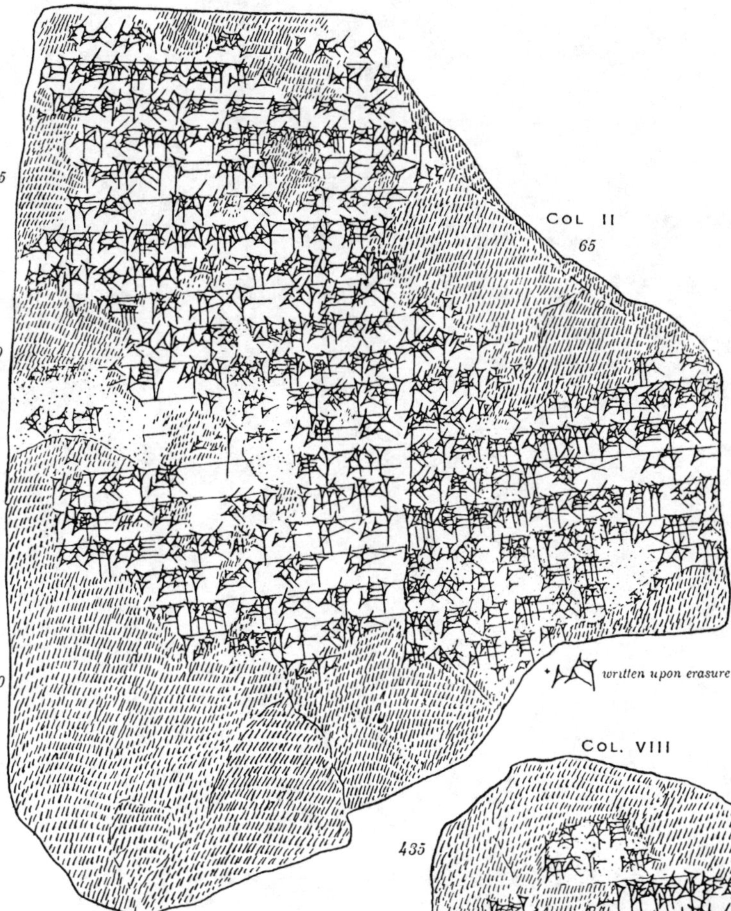
Col. I
Col. II
written upon erasure

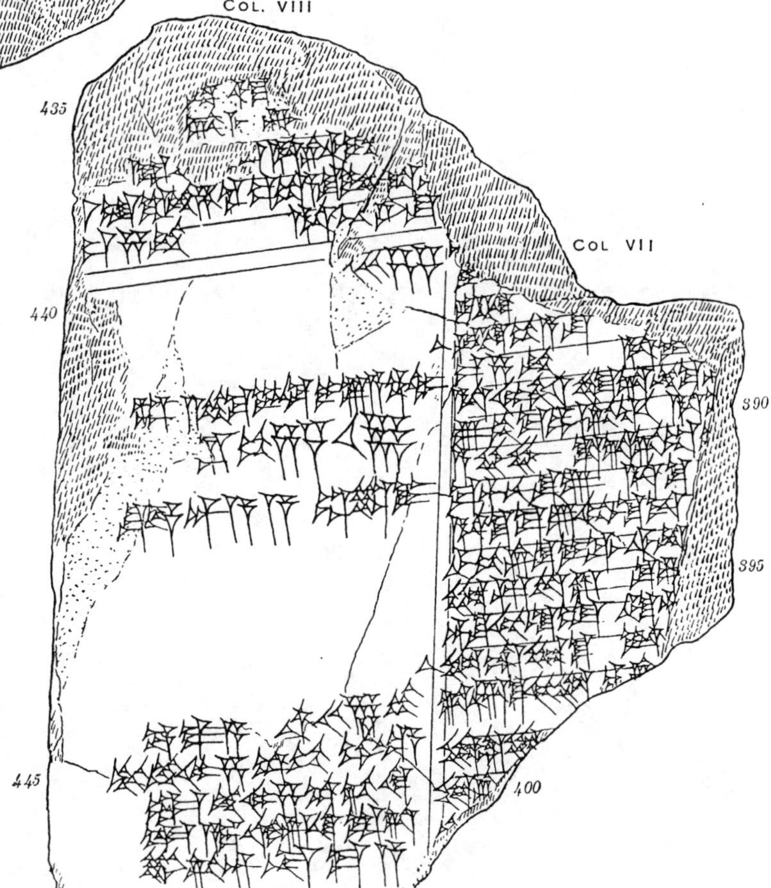
Col. VIII
Col VII

2

Col. I   Col. II

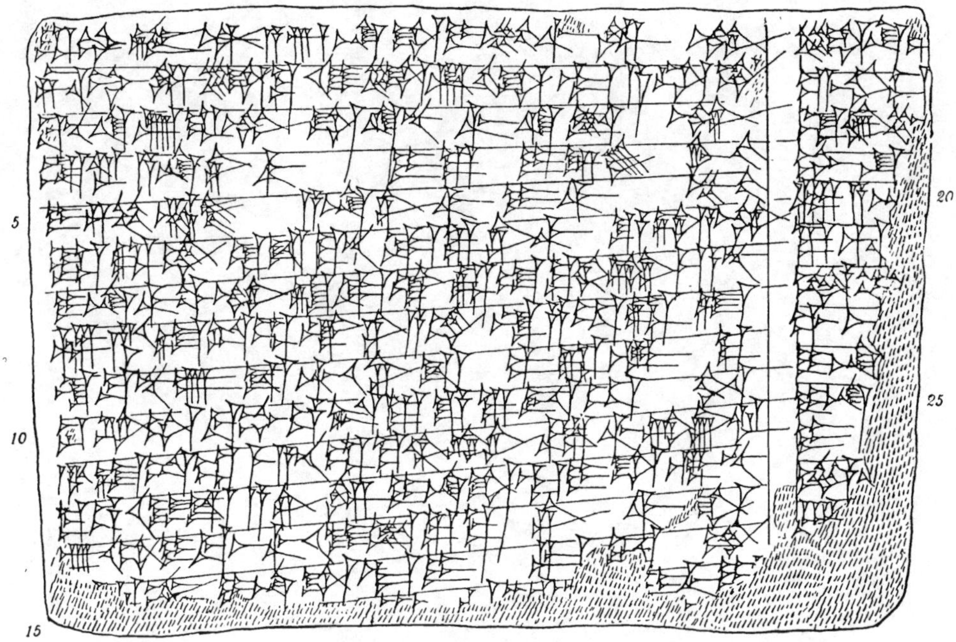

Col. VI   Col. V

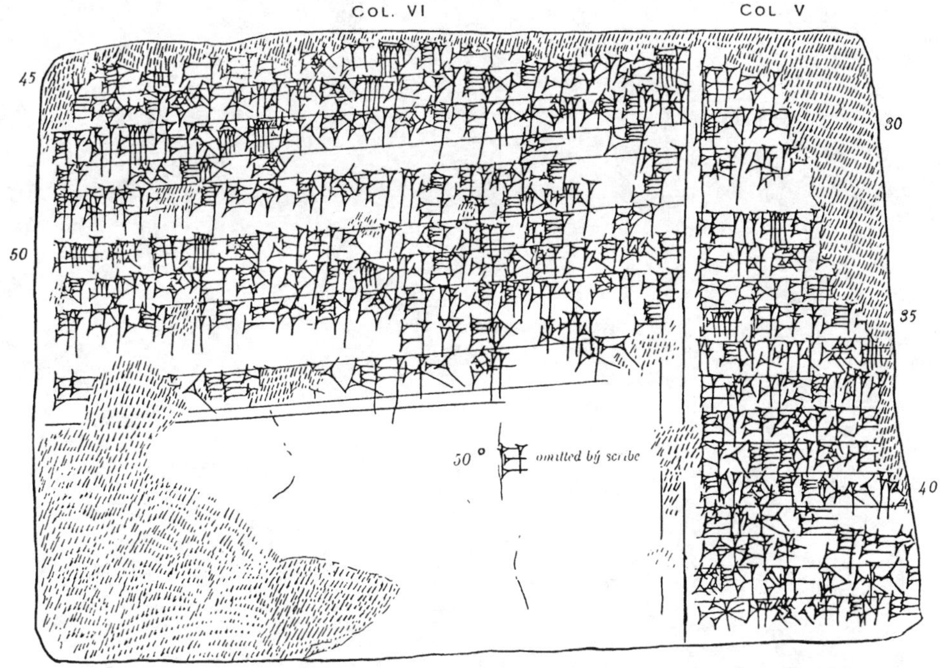

3

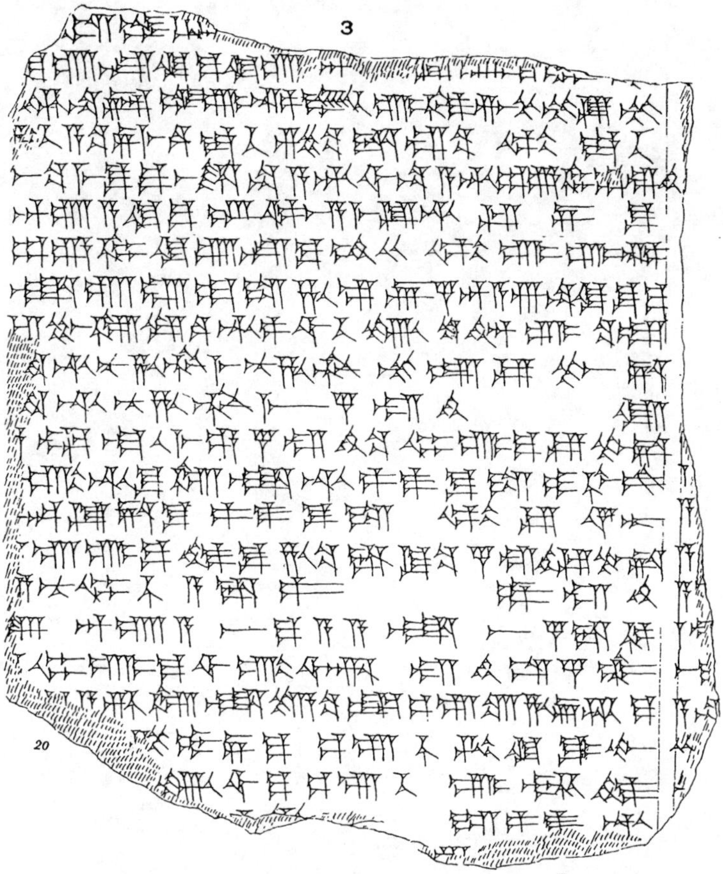

4

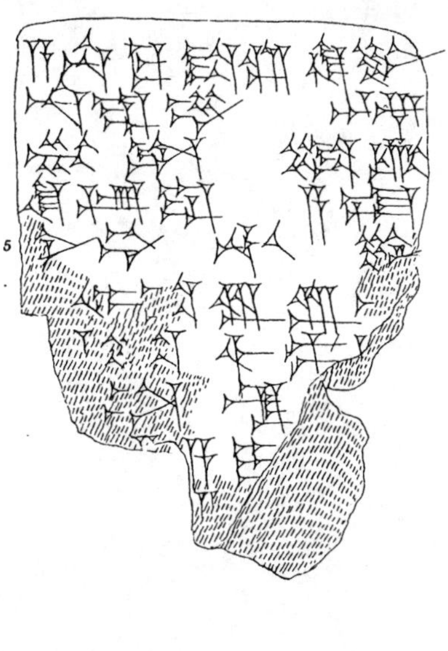

5

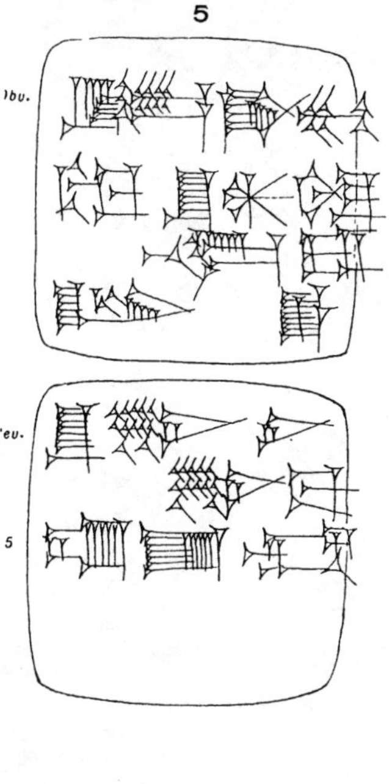

obv.

rev.

6

Obv.

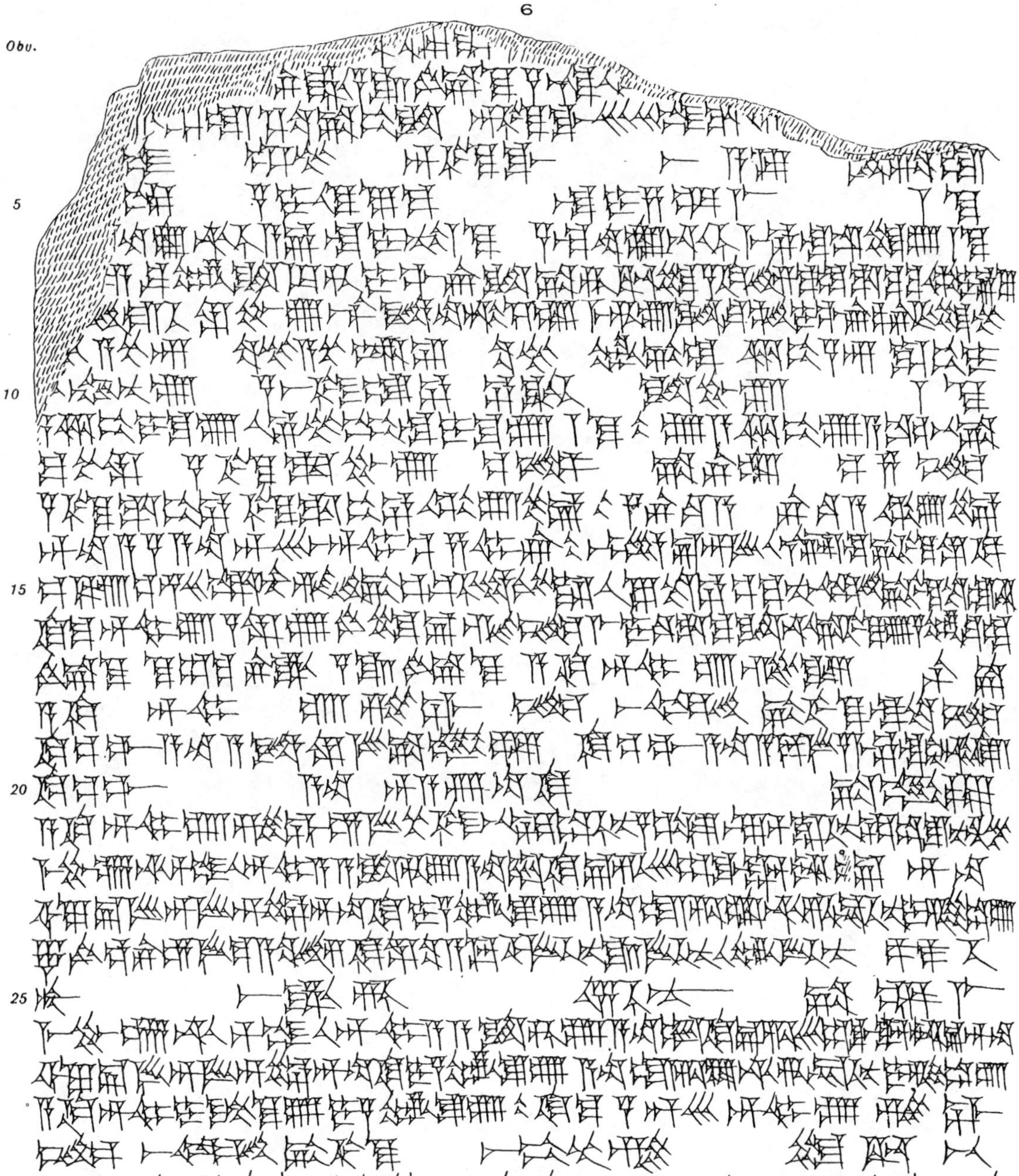

° Erasure.

6 CONTINUED

Rev.

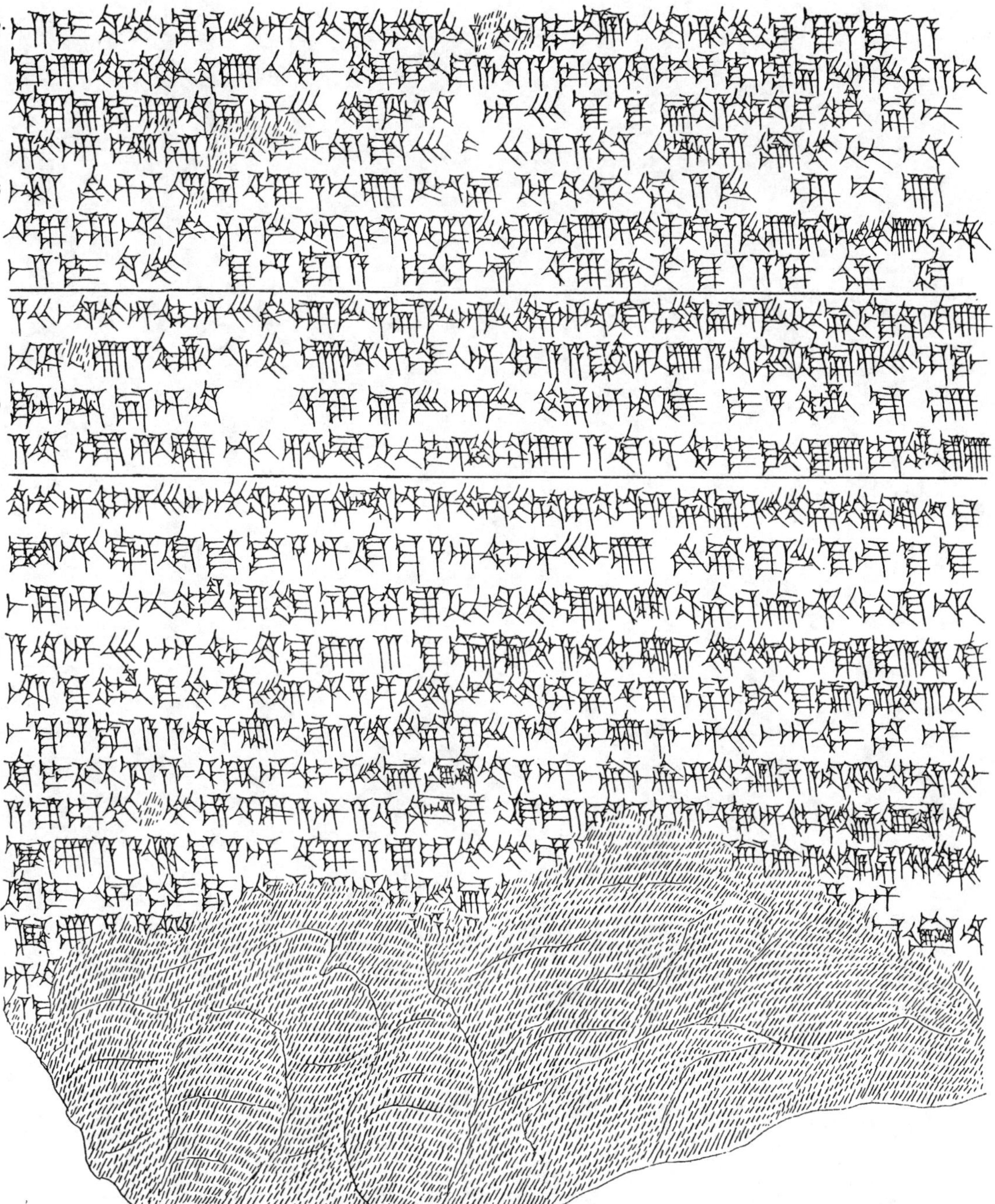

7

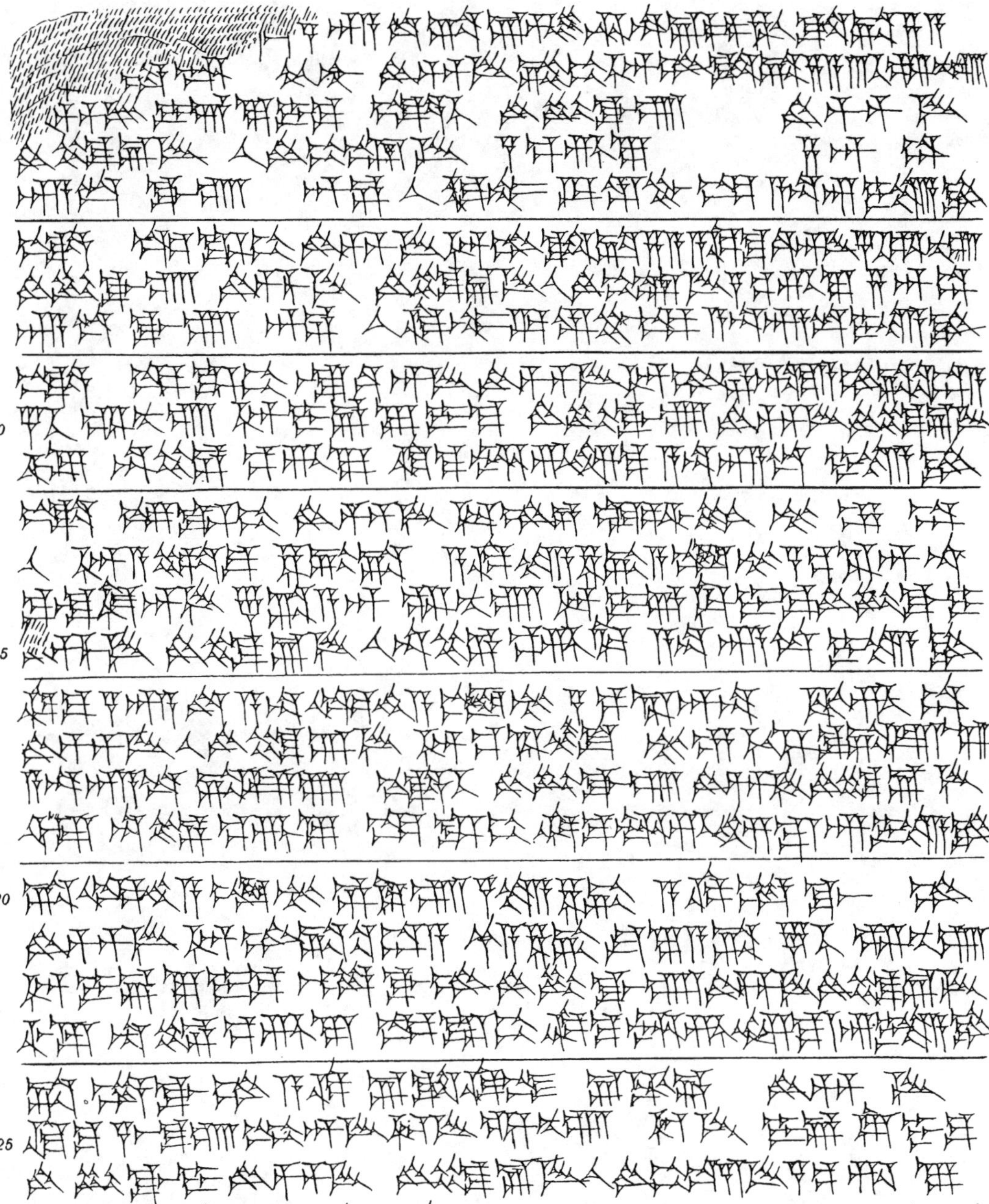

7 CONTINUED

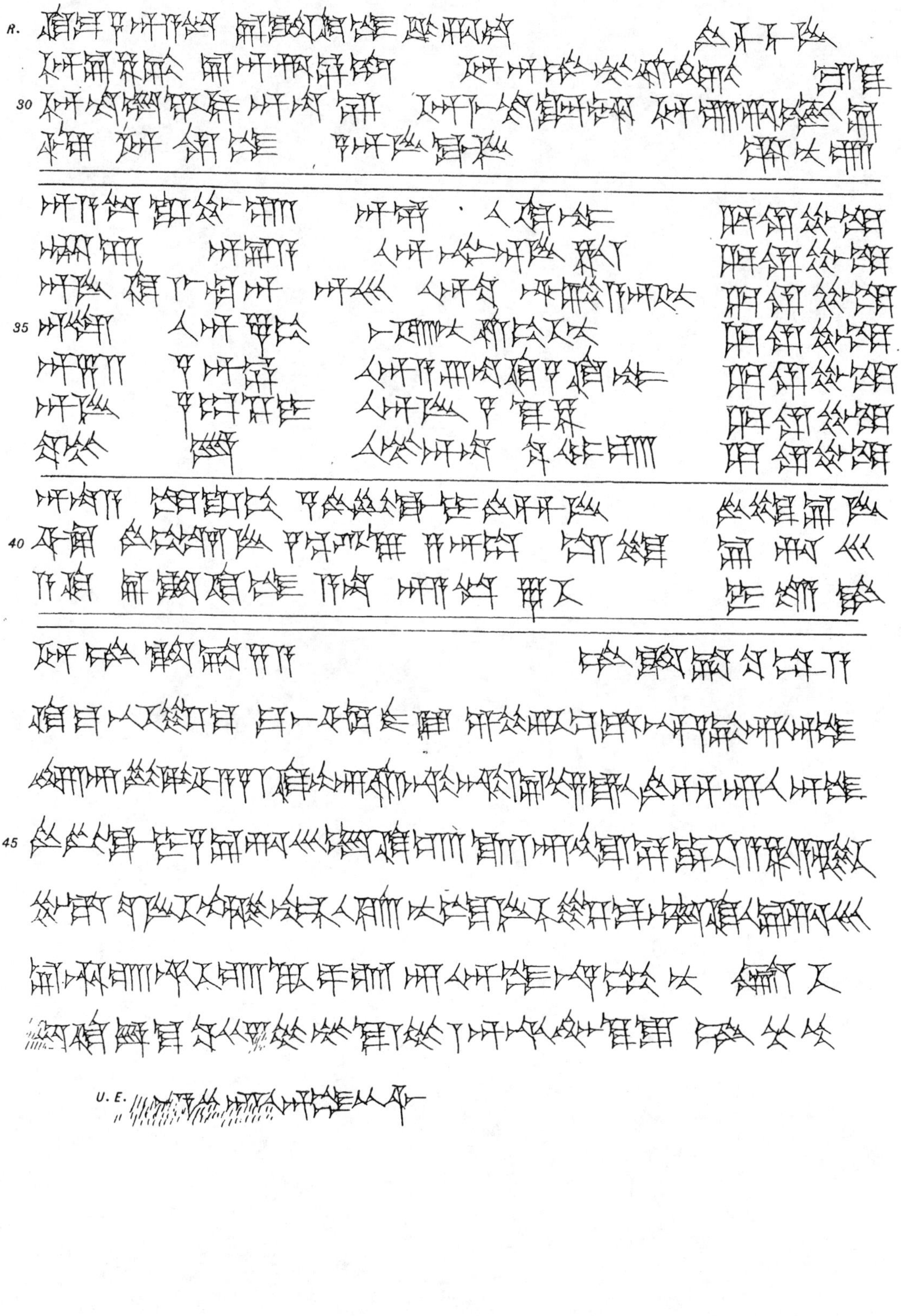

8

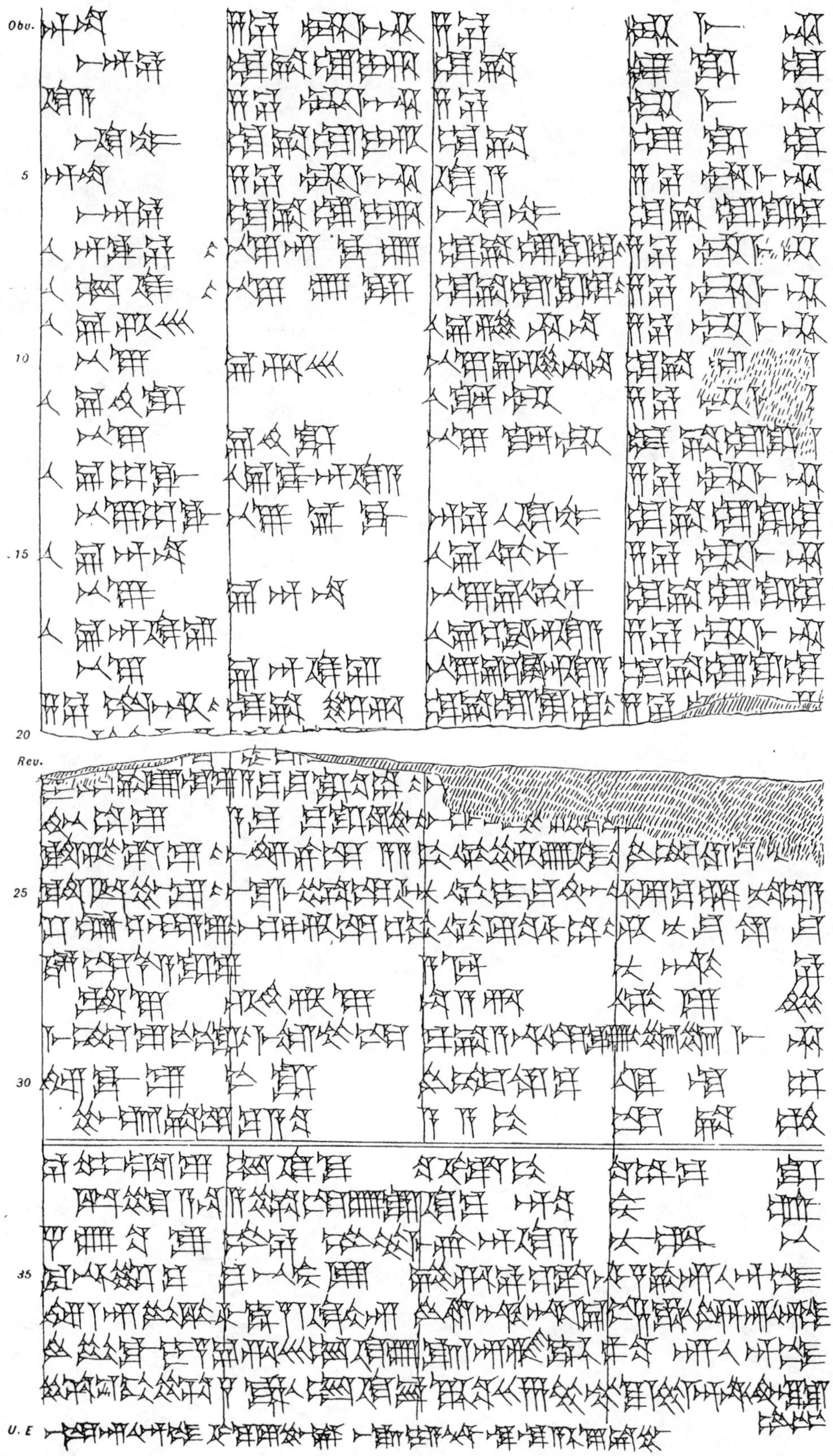

9

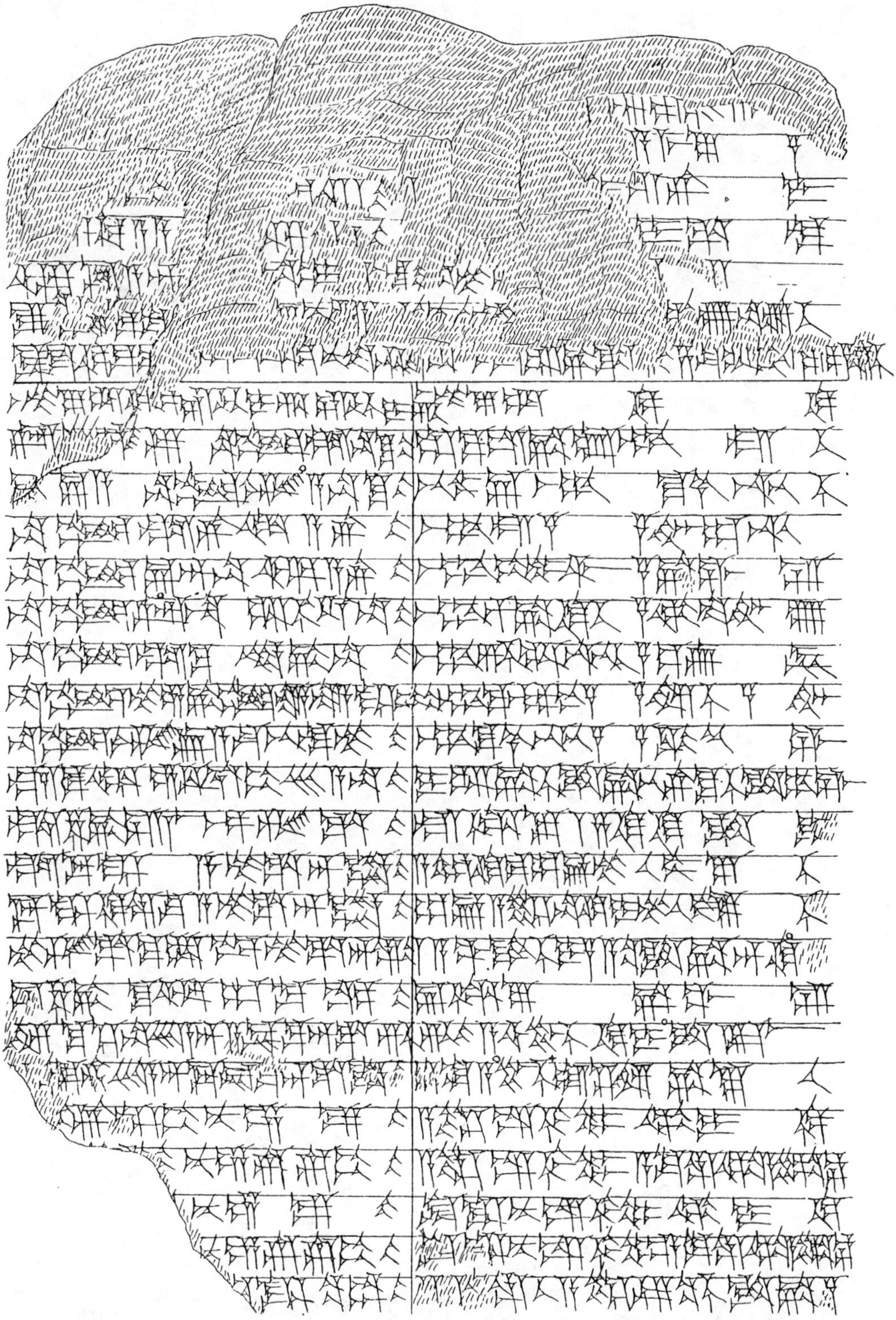

10 ° omitted by scribe.

13 ° Mistake of scribe for

21 ° Mistake of scribe for

23 ° omitted by scribe.

24 ° omitted by scribe. + omitted by scribe.

9 CONTNUED

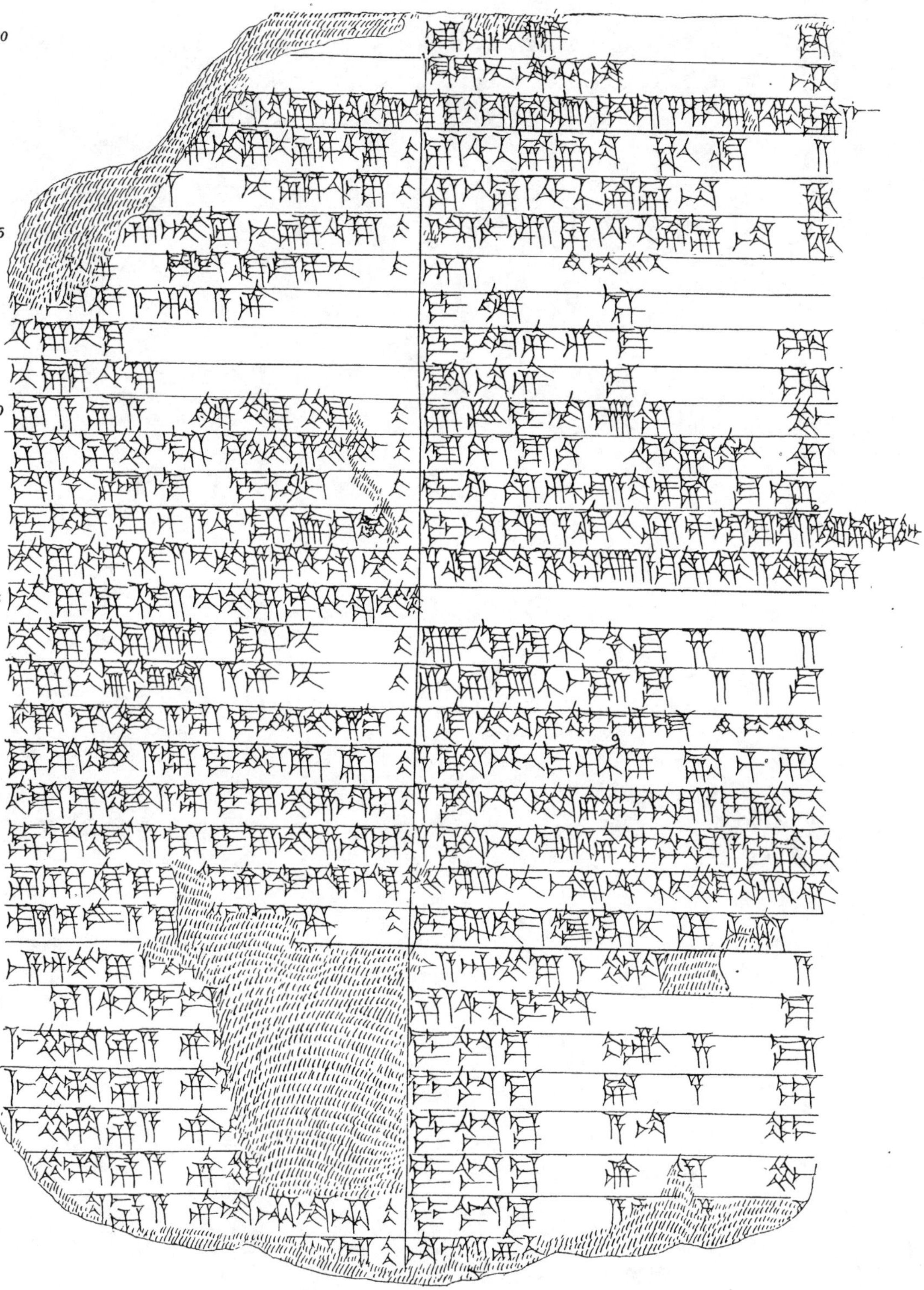

43 ° rest mistake of scribe. 49 ° omitted by scribe.

47 ° Mistake of scribe for

10

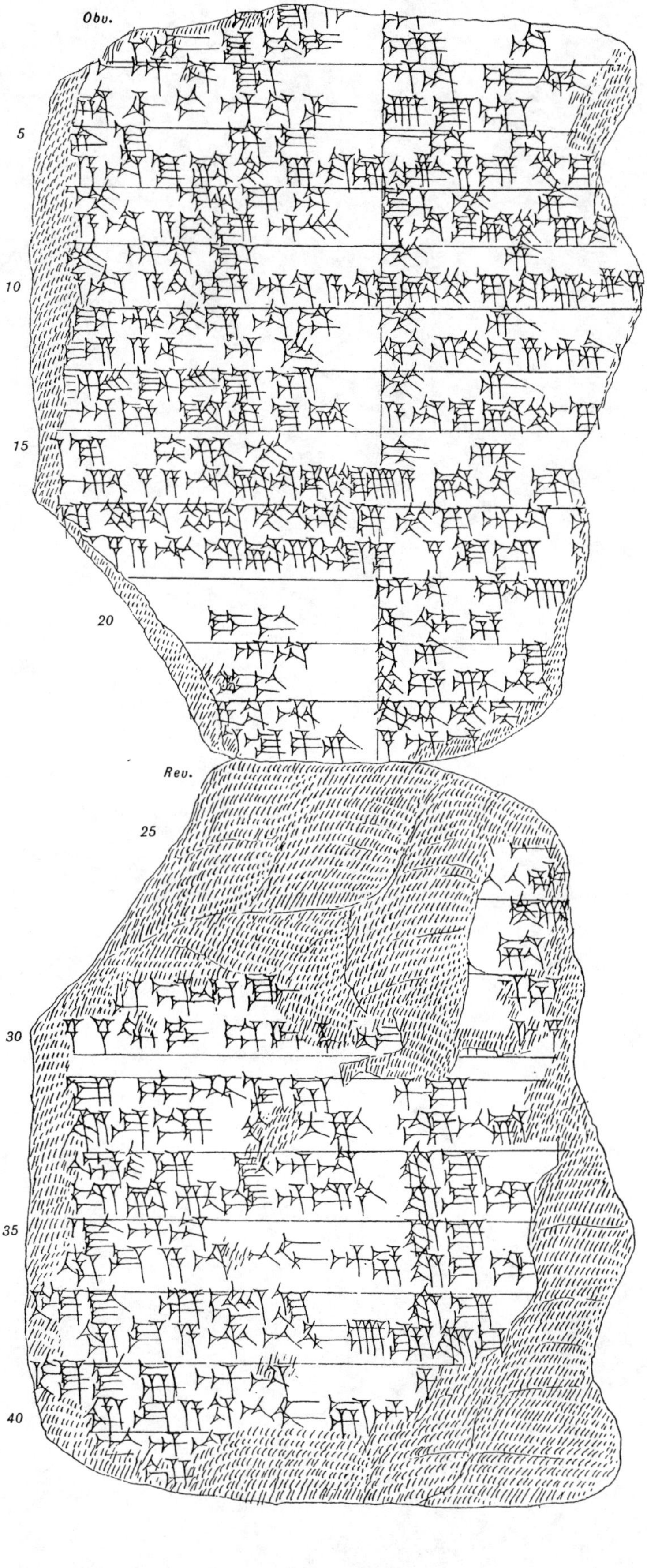

11

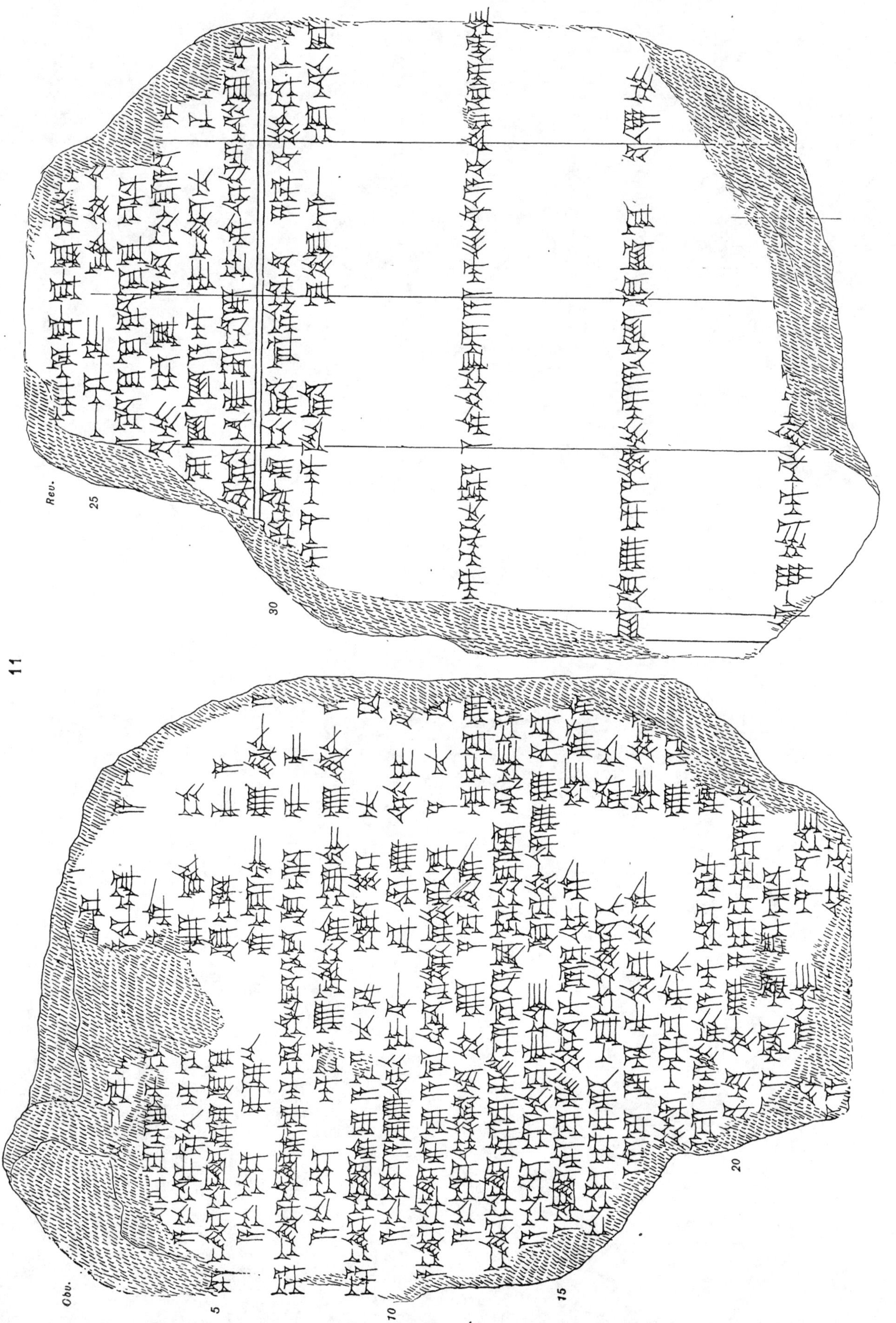

12

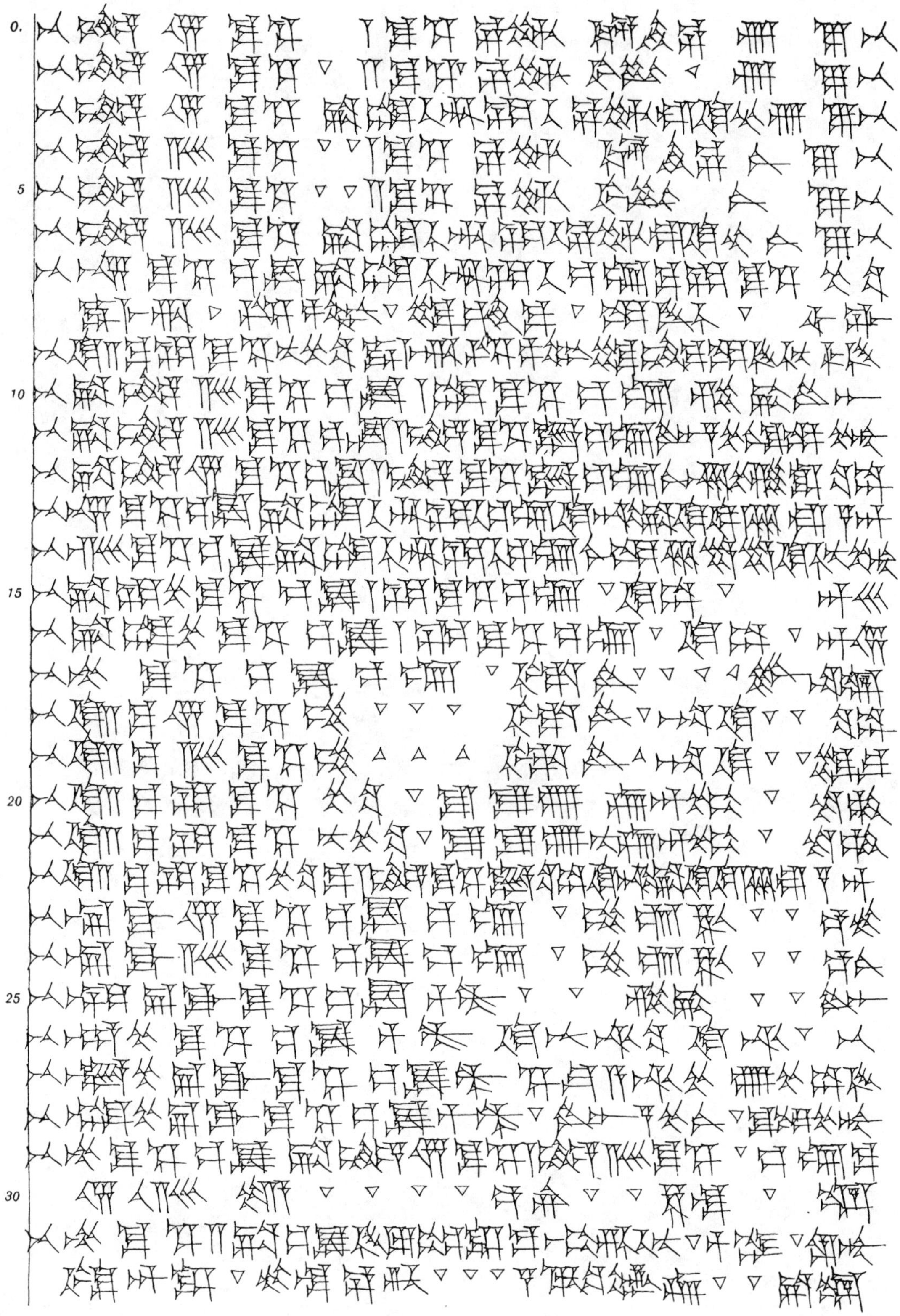

° *omitted.*

12 CONTINUED

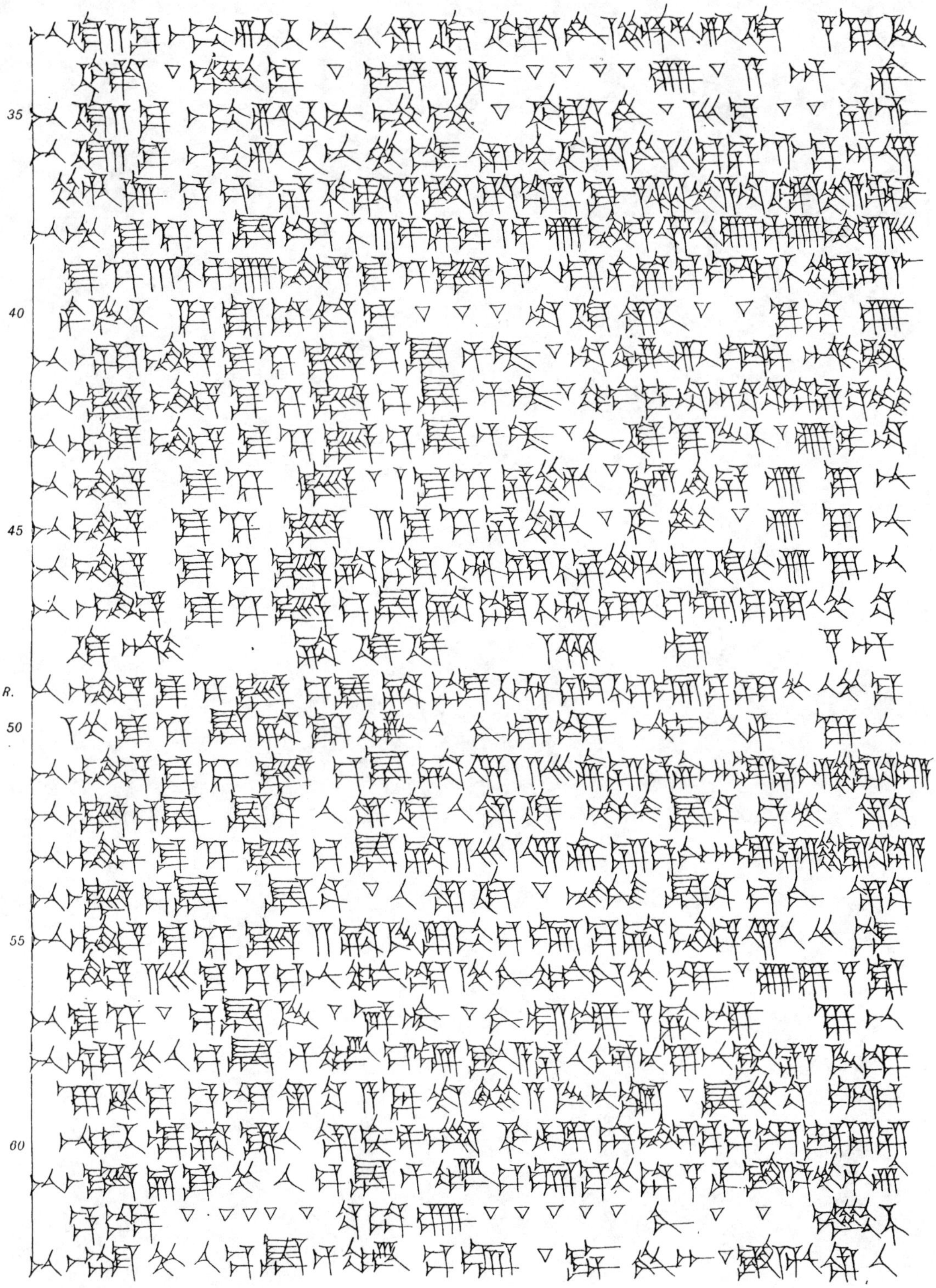

12 CONTINUED

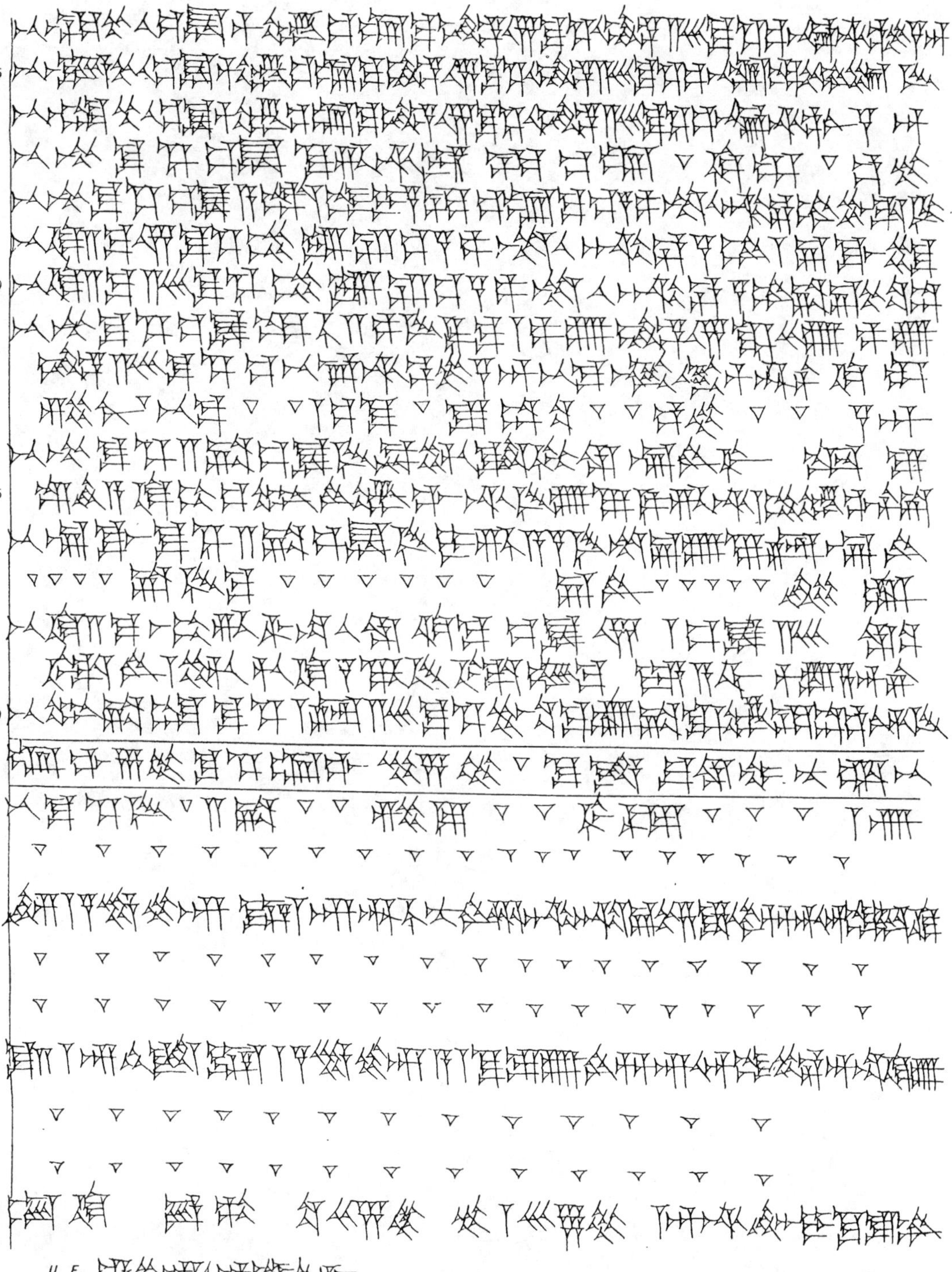

U. E.

13

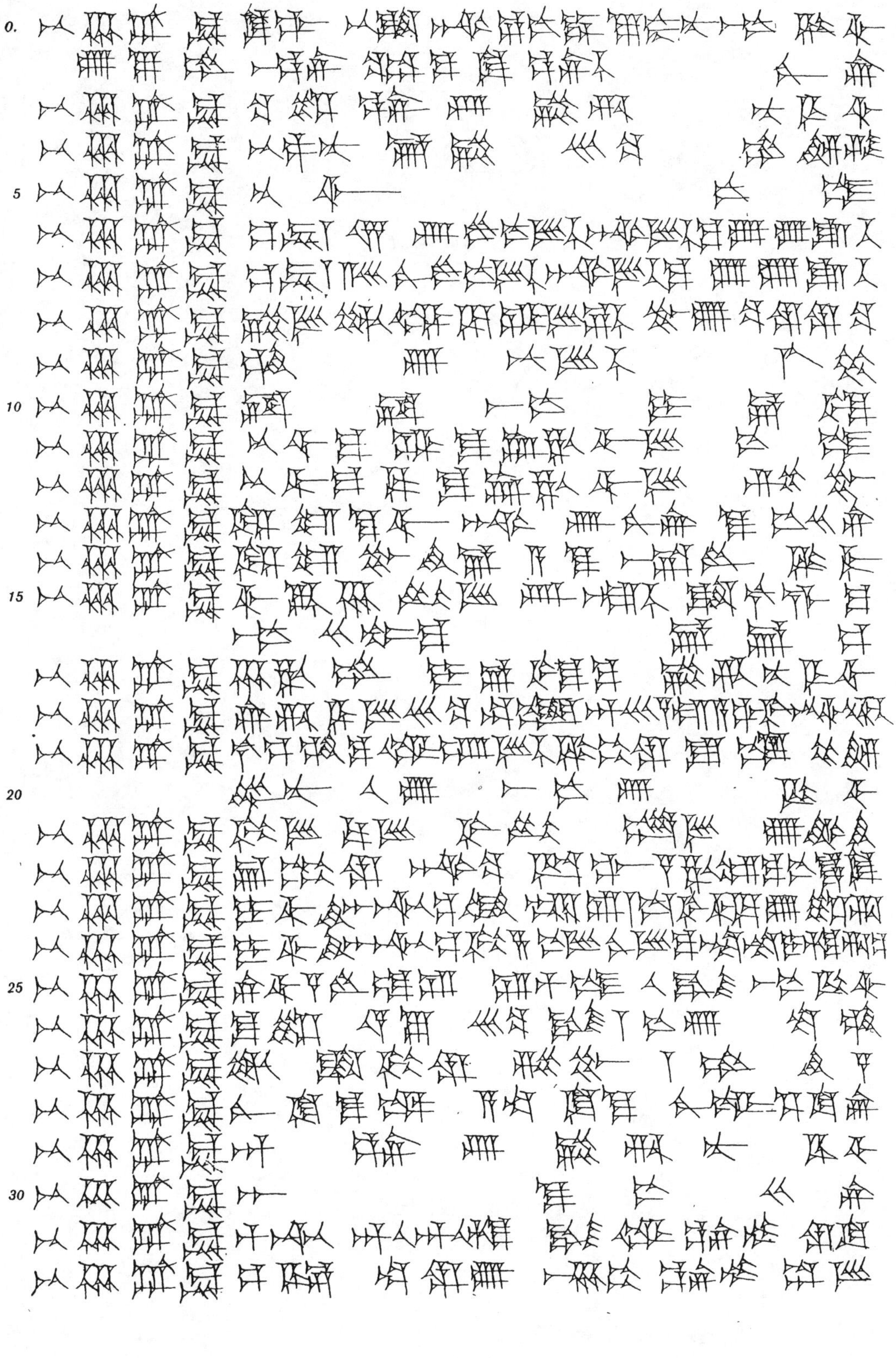

13 CONTINUED

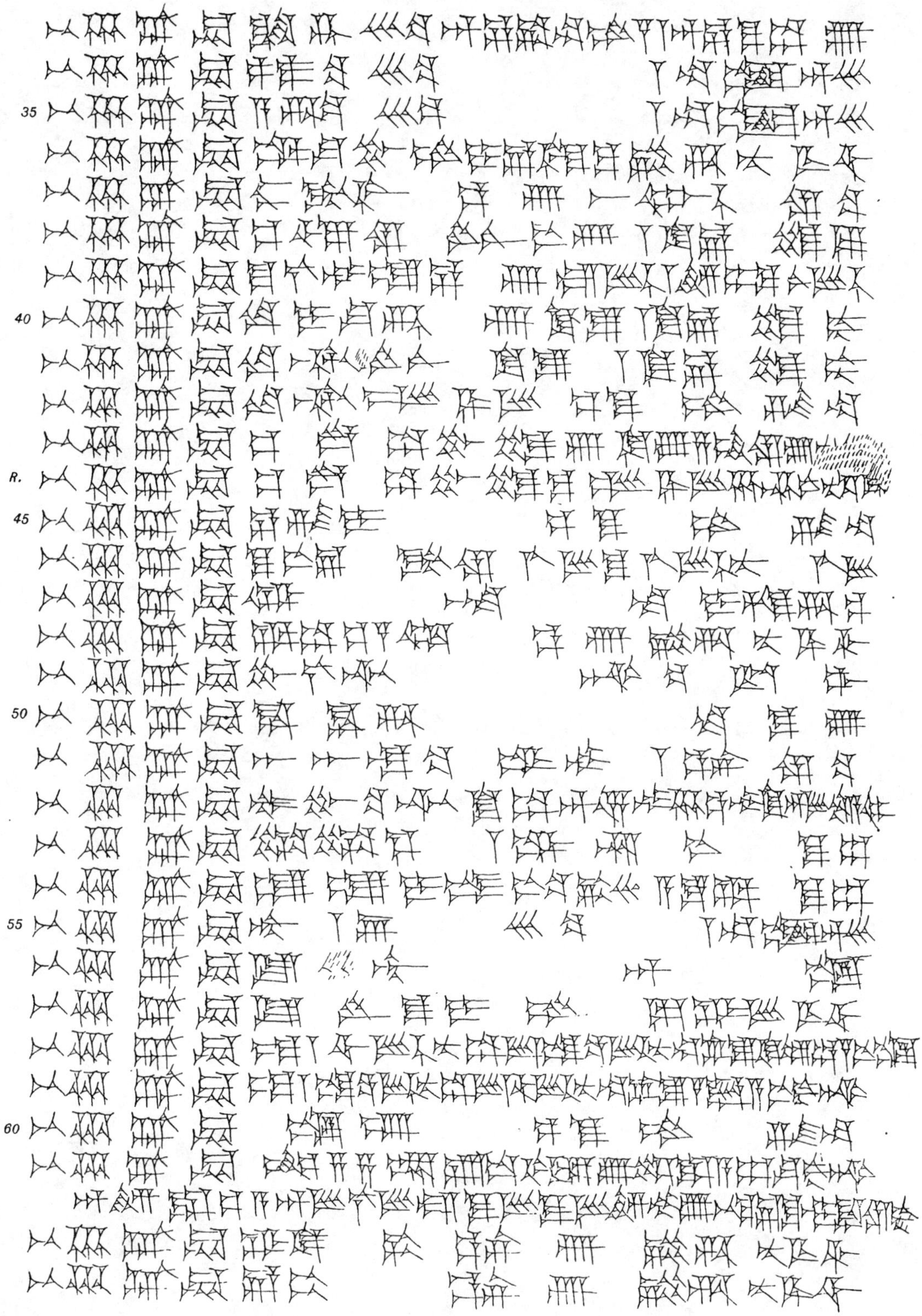

13 CONTINUED

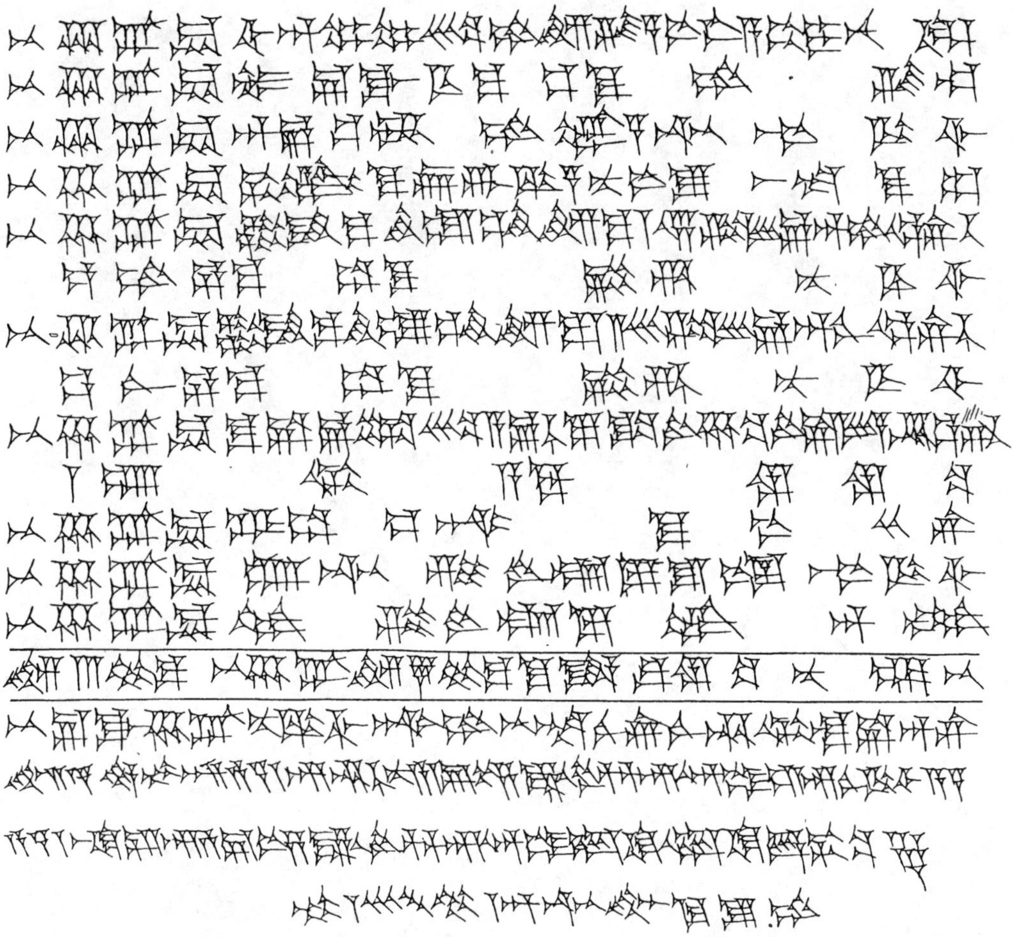

U. E. 

14

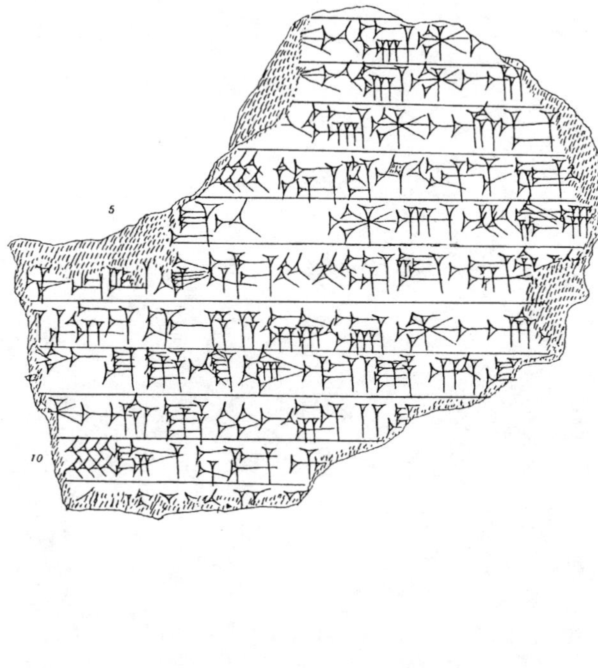

15

everse.

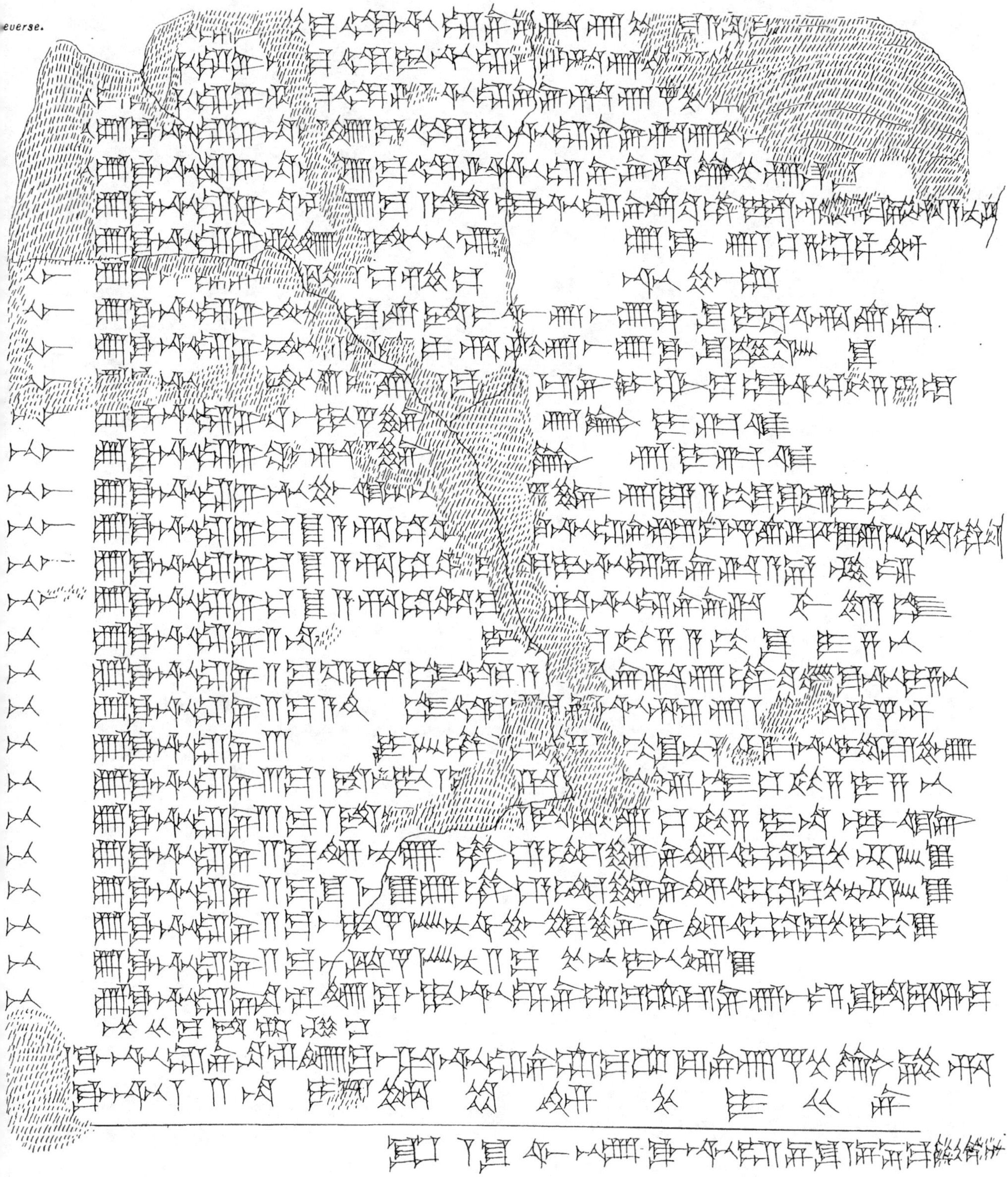

16

Reverse.

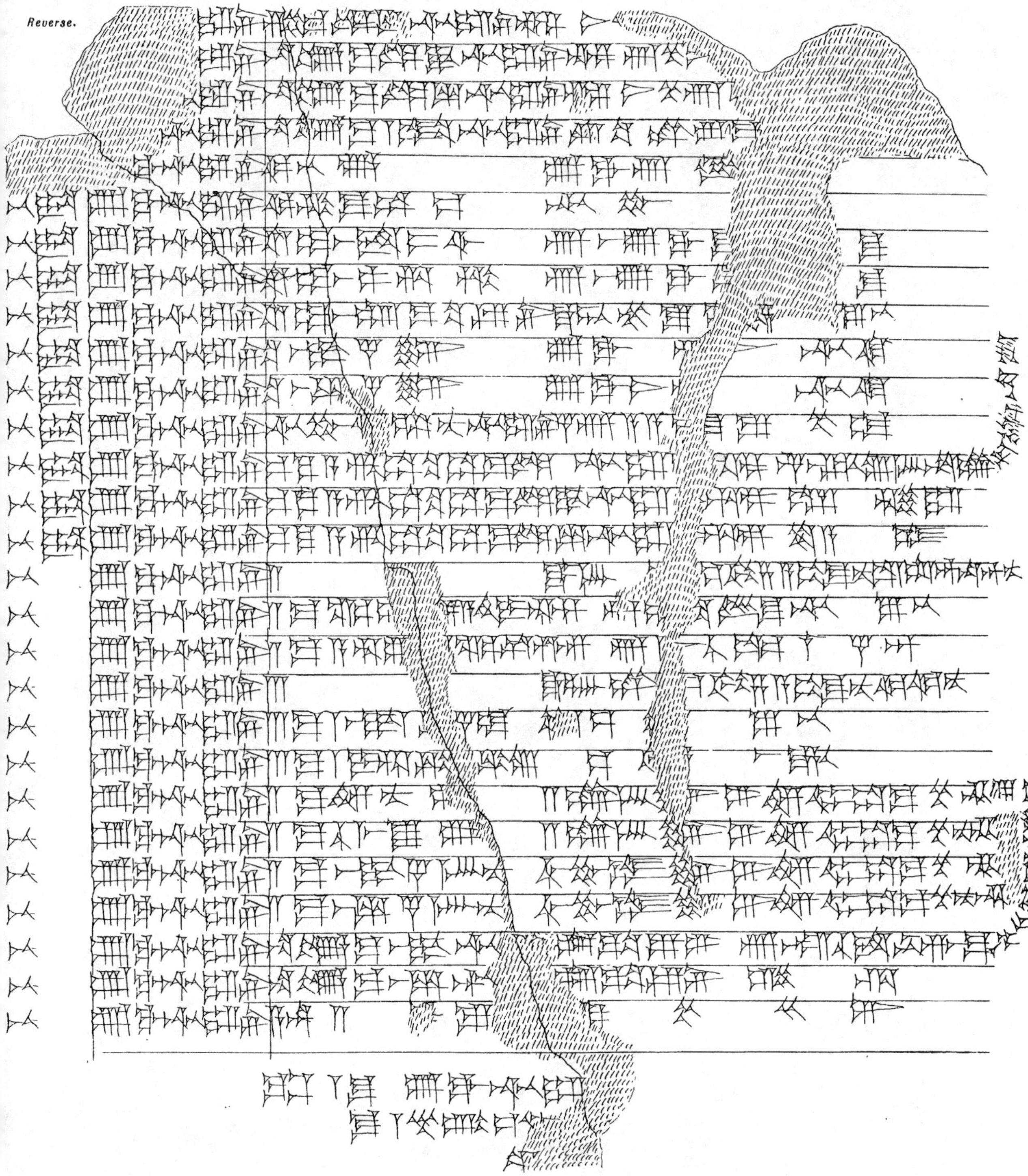

17

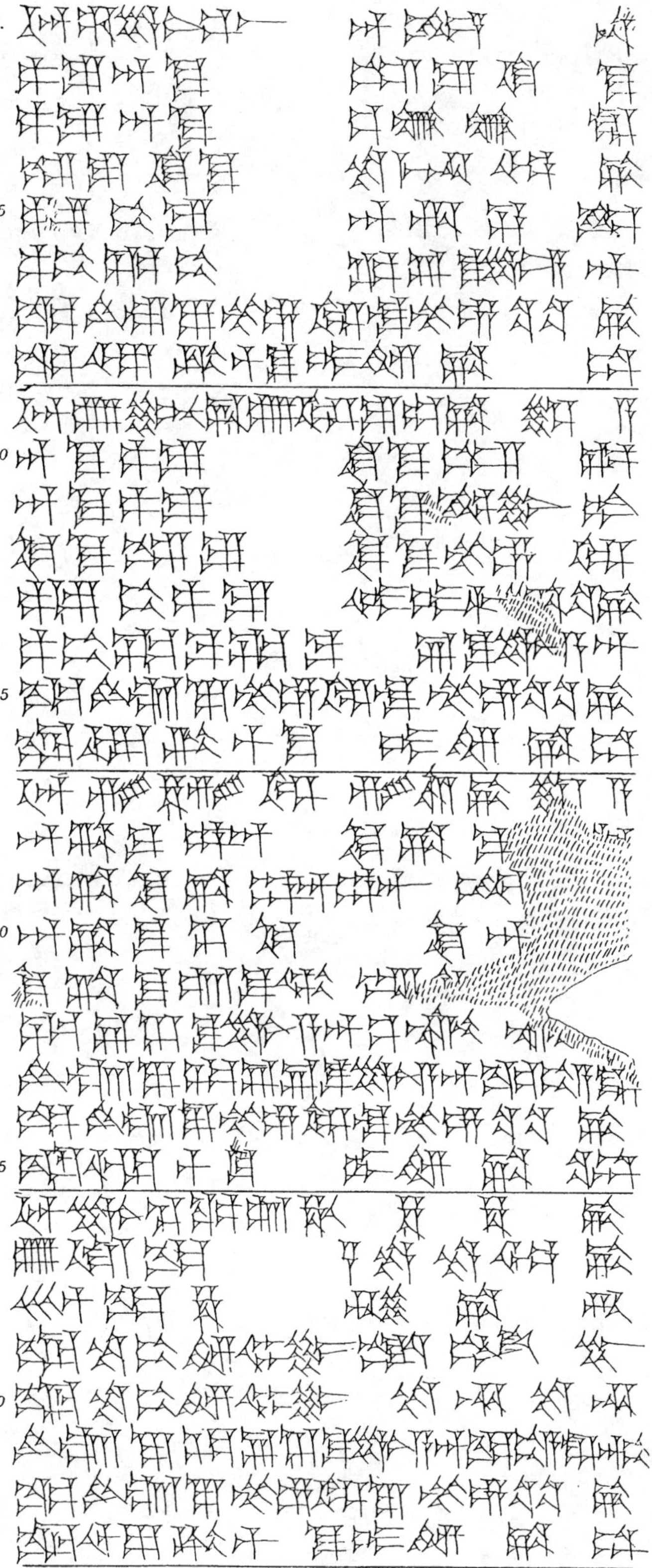

18

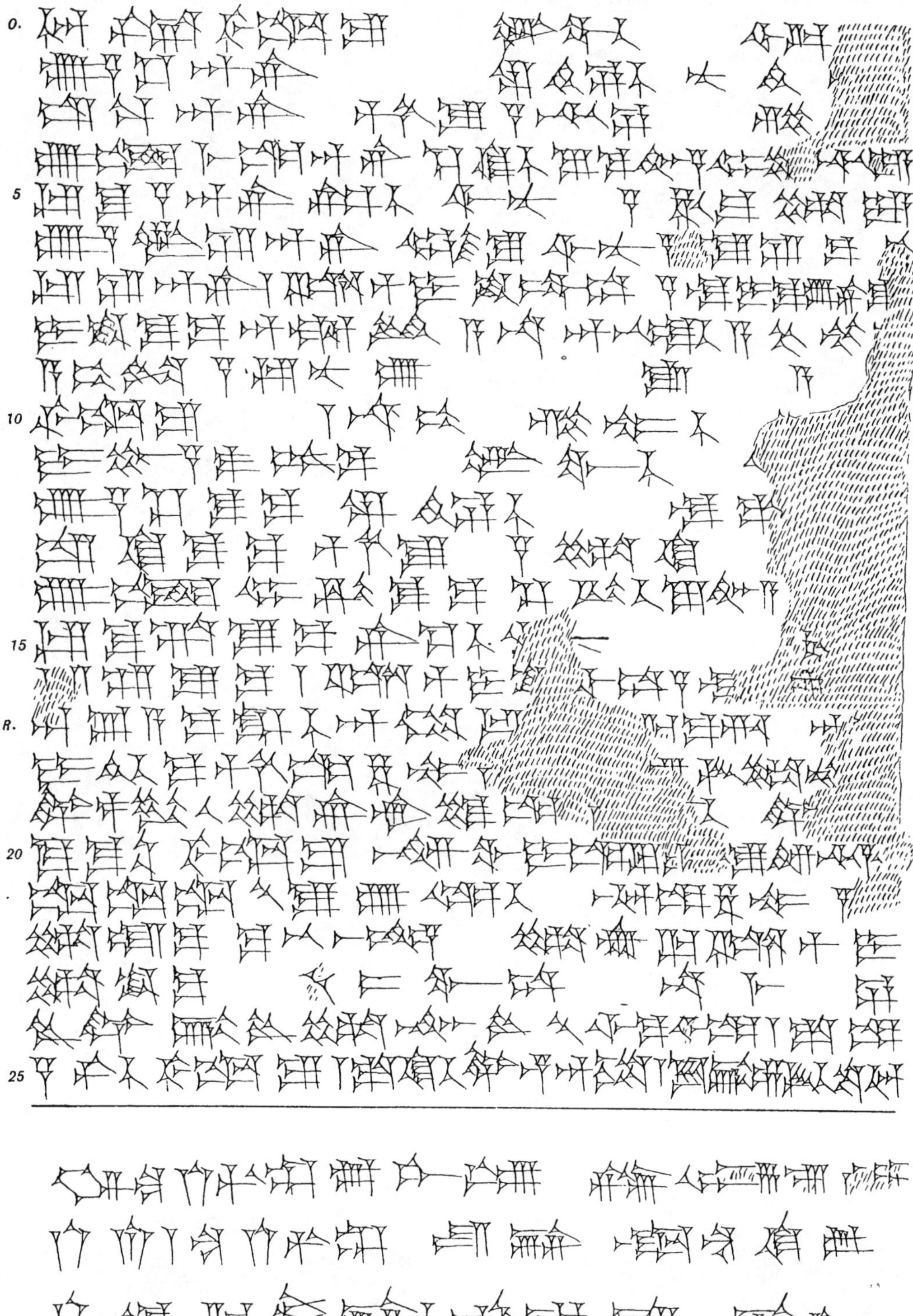

19

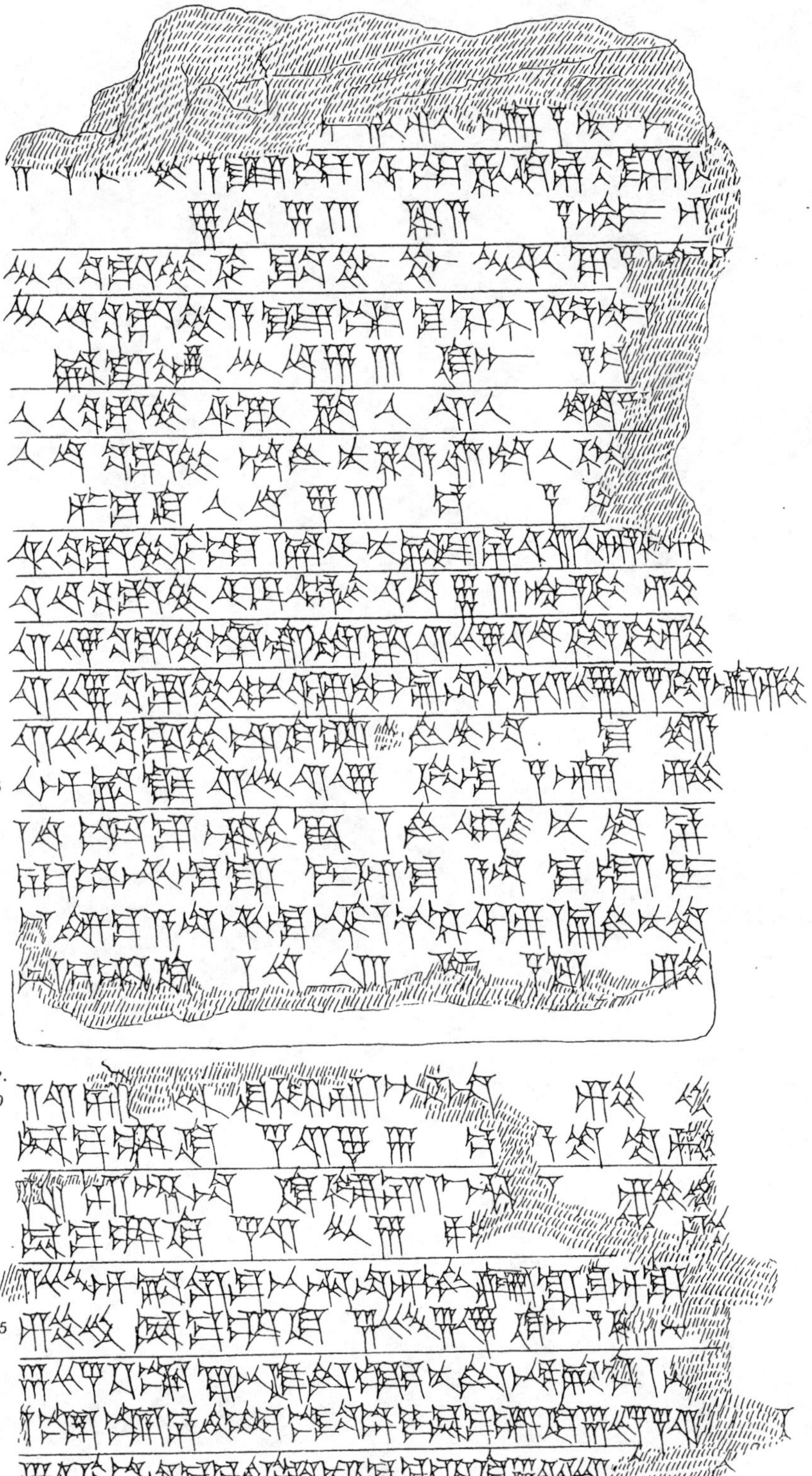

R.

19 CONTINUED

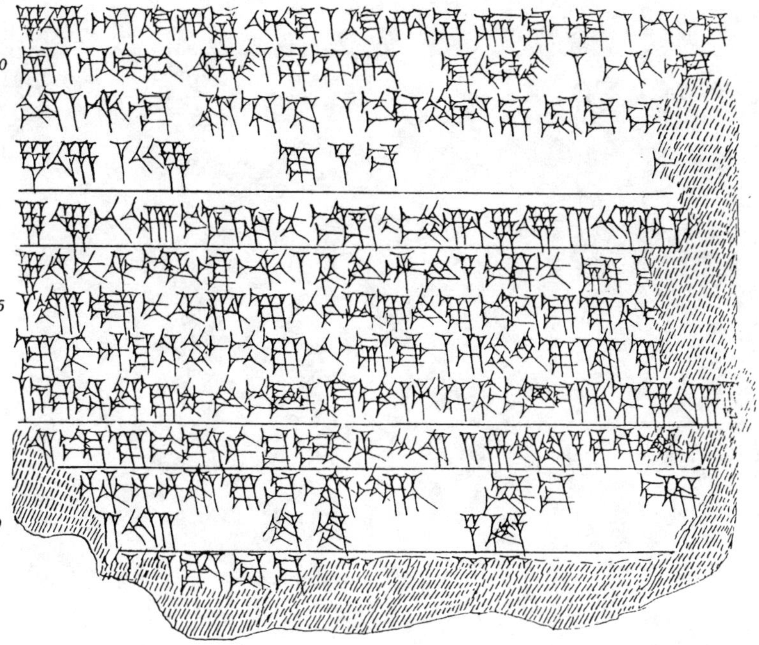

20

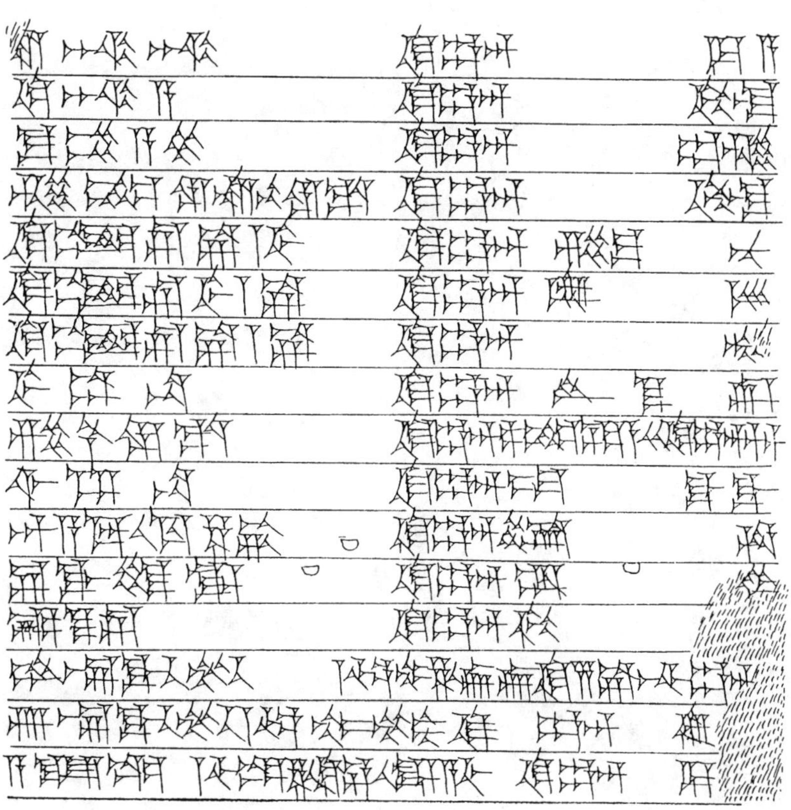

20 CONTINUED

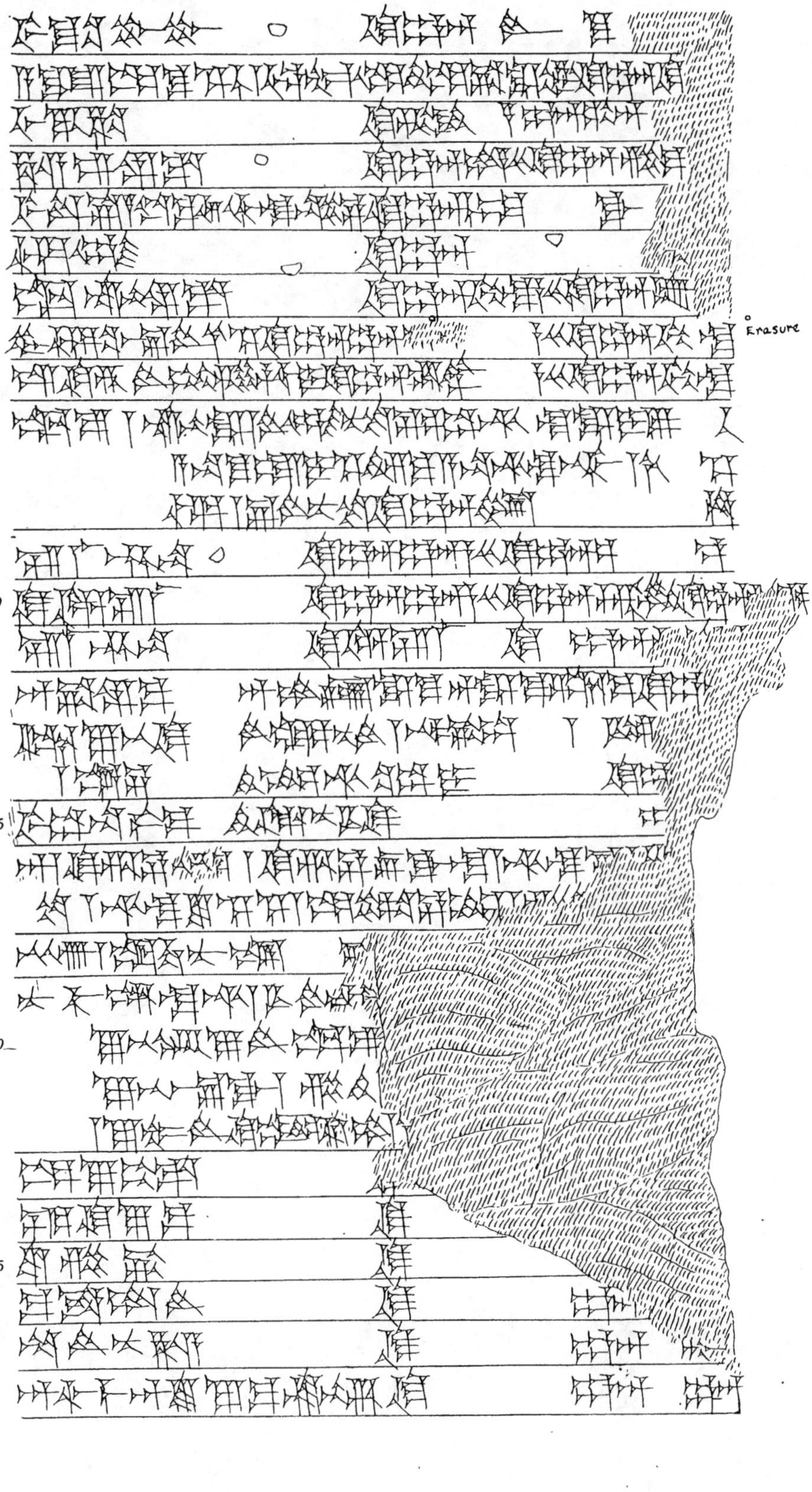

R.

20 CONTINUED

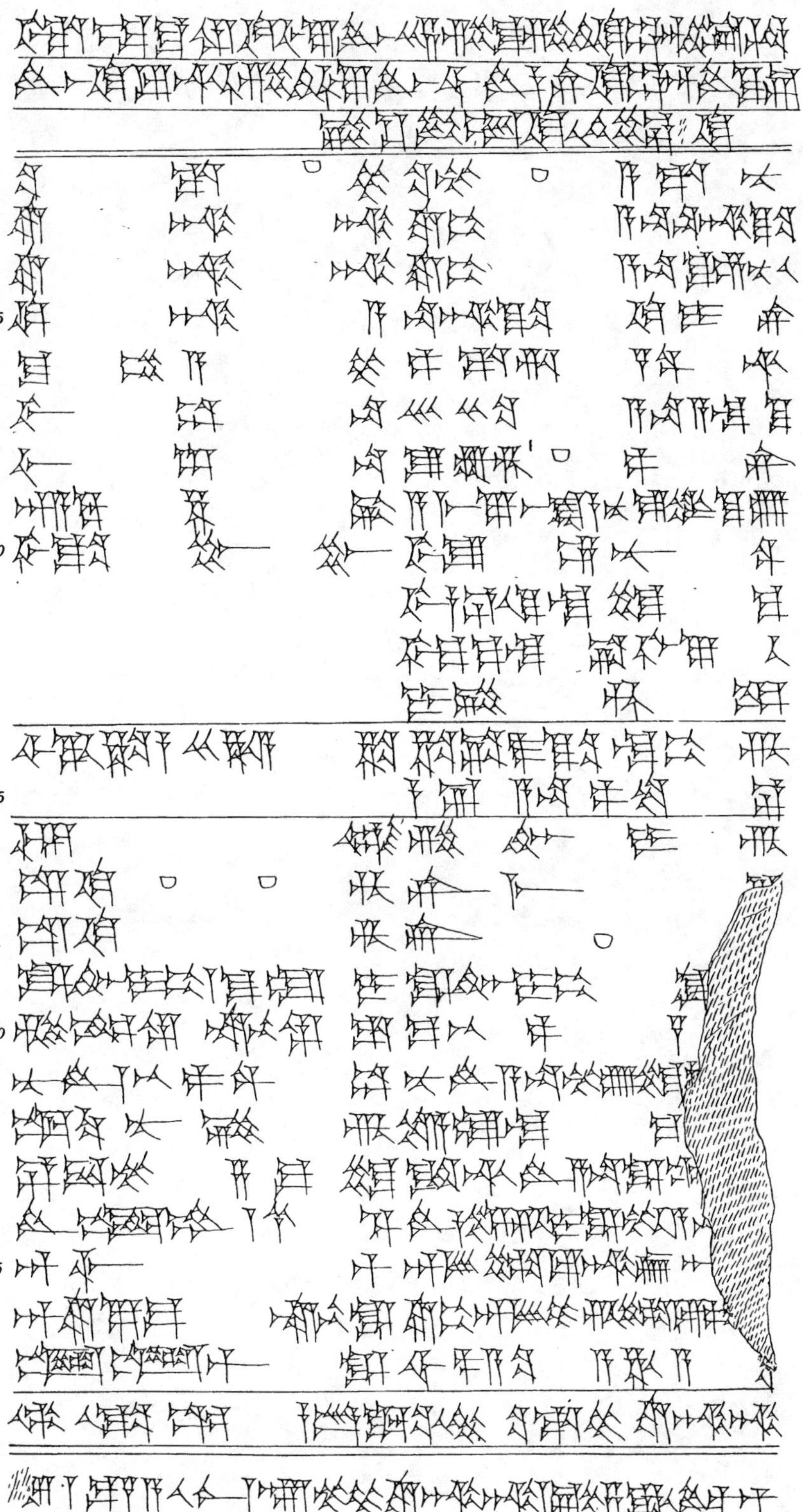

21

O.

R.

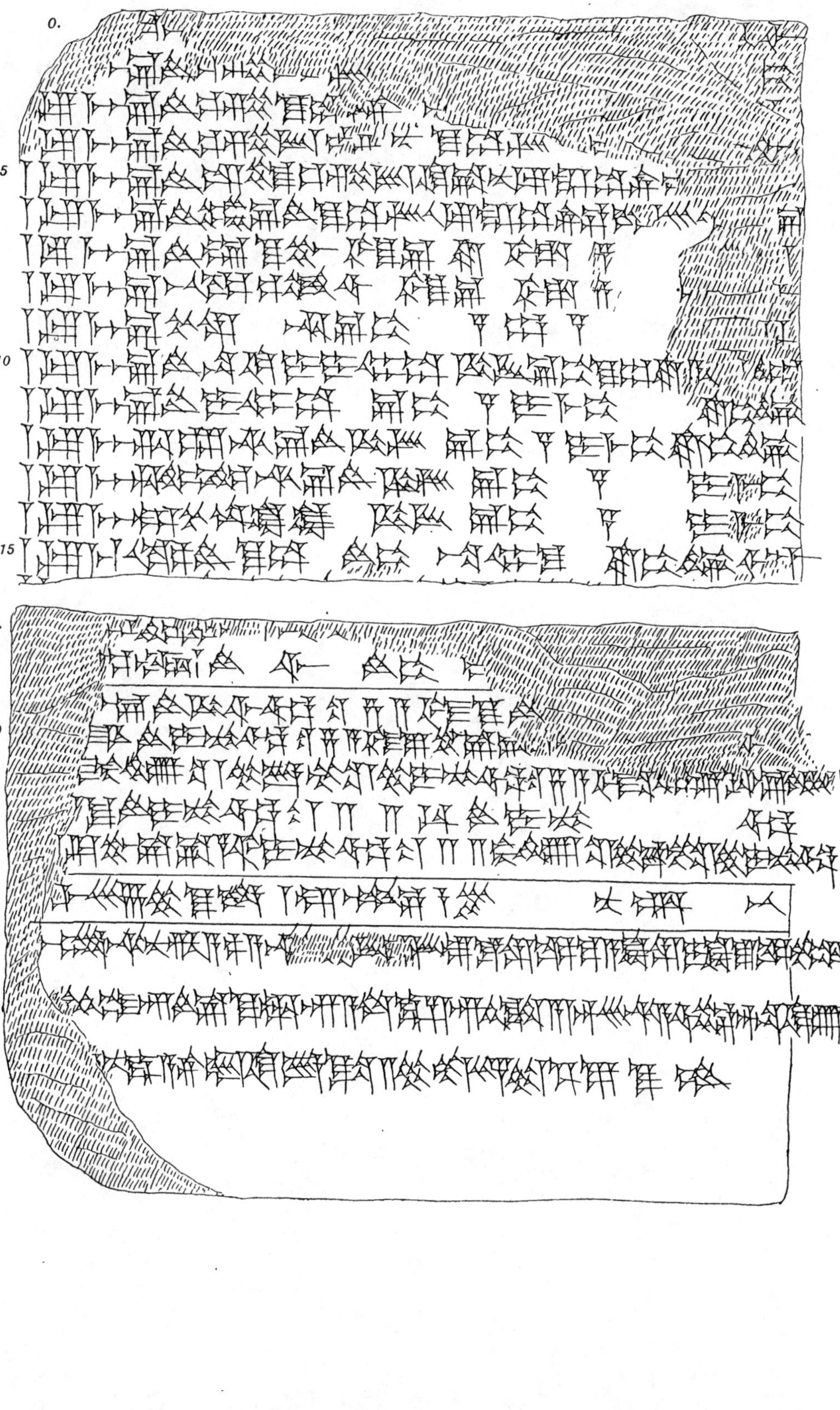

22

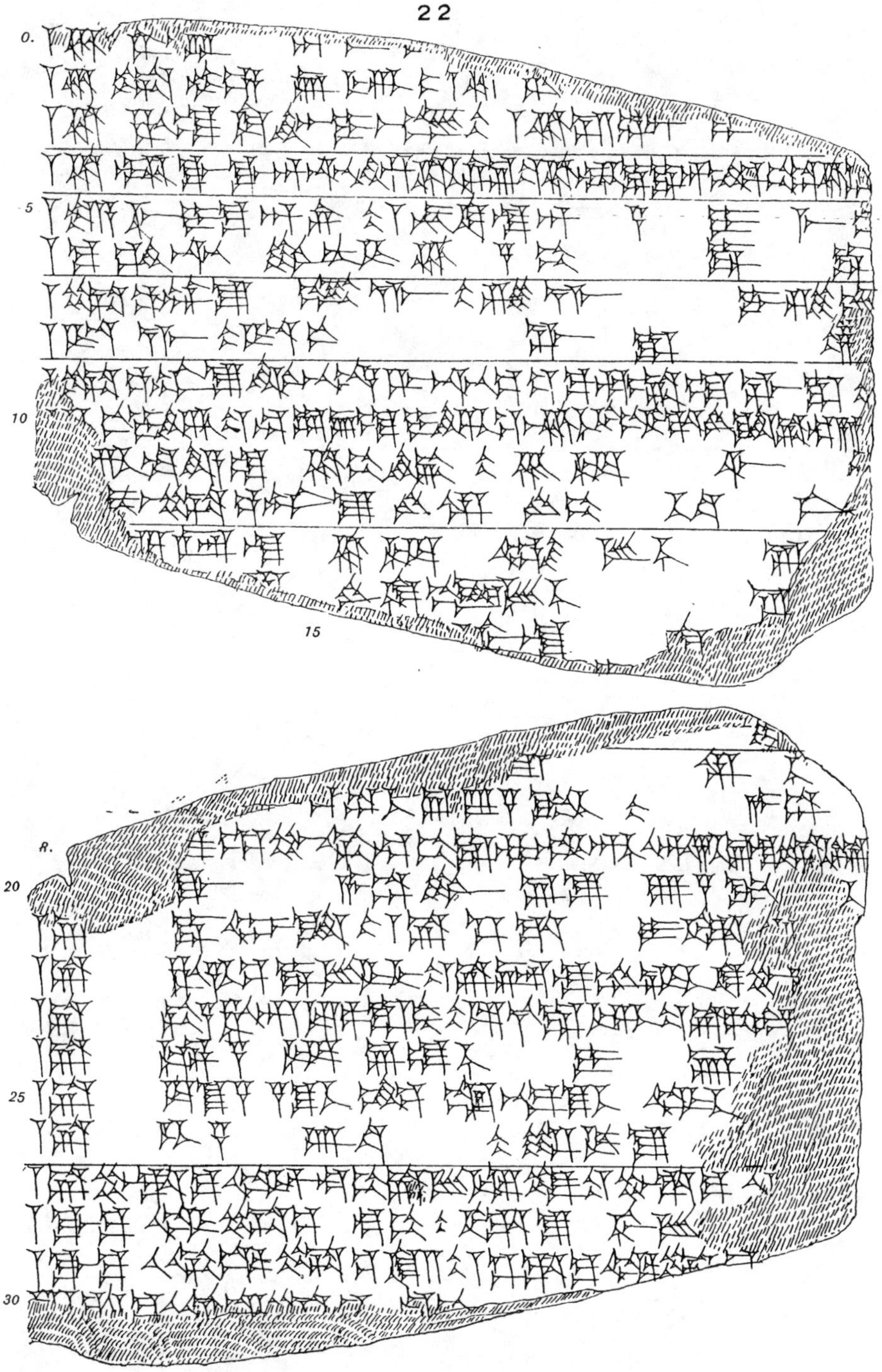

23

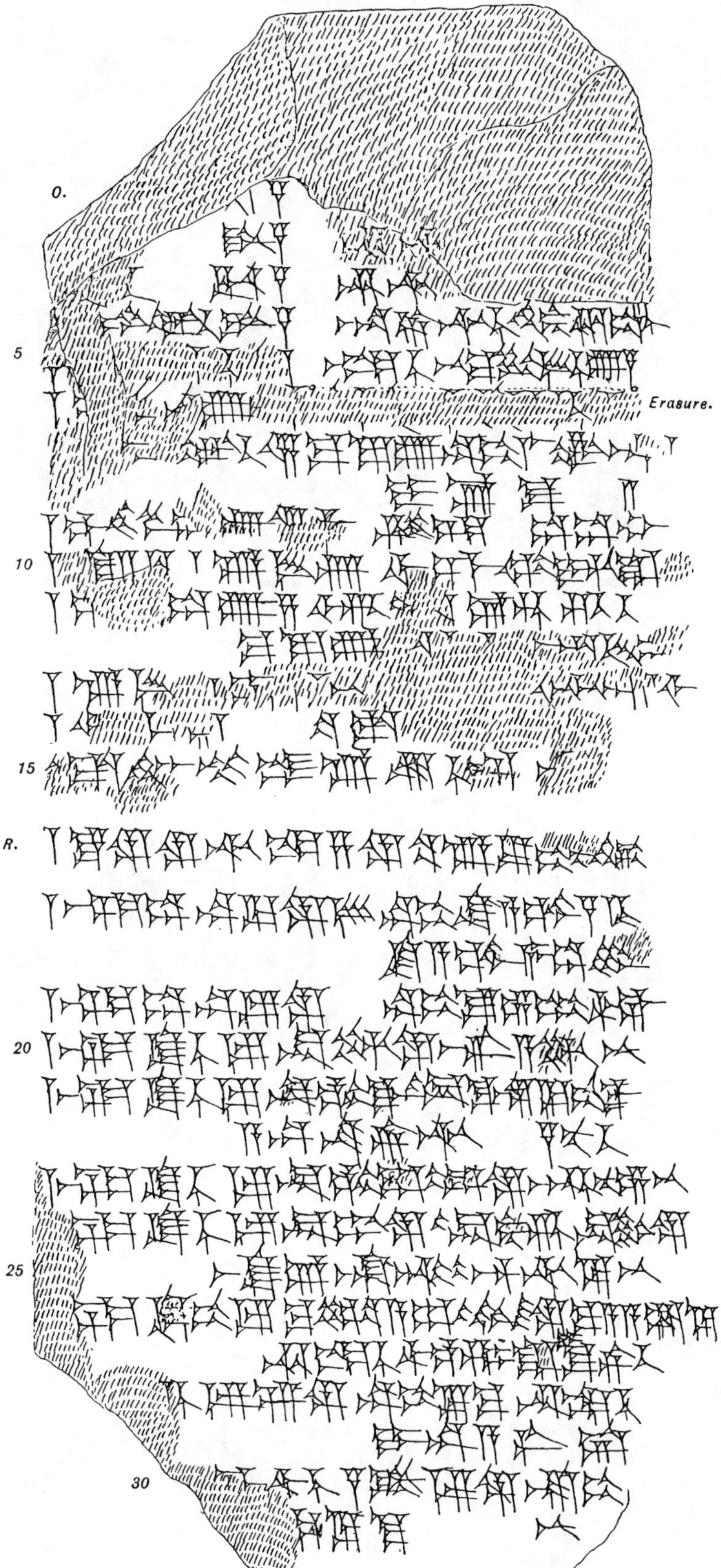

24

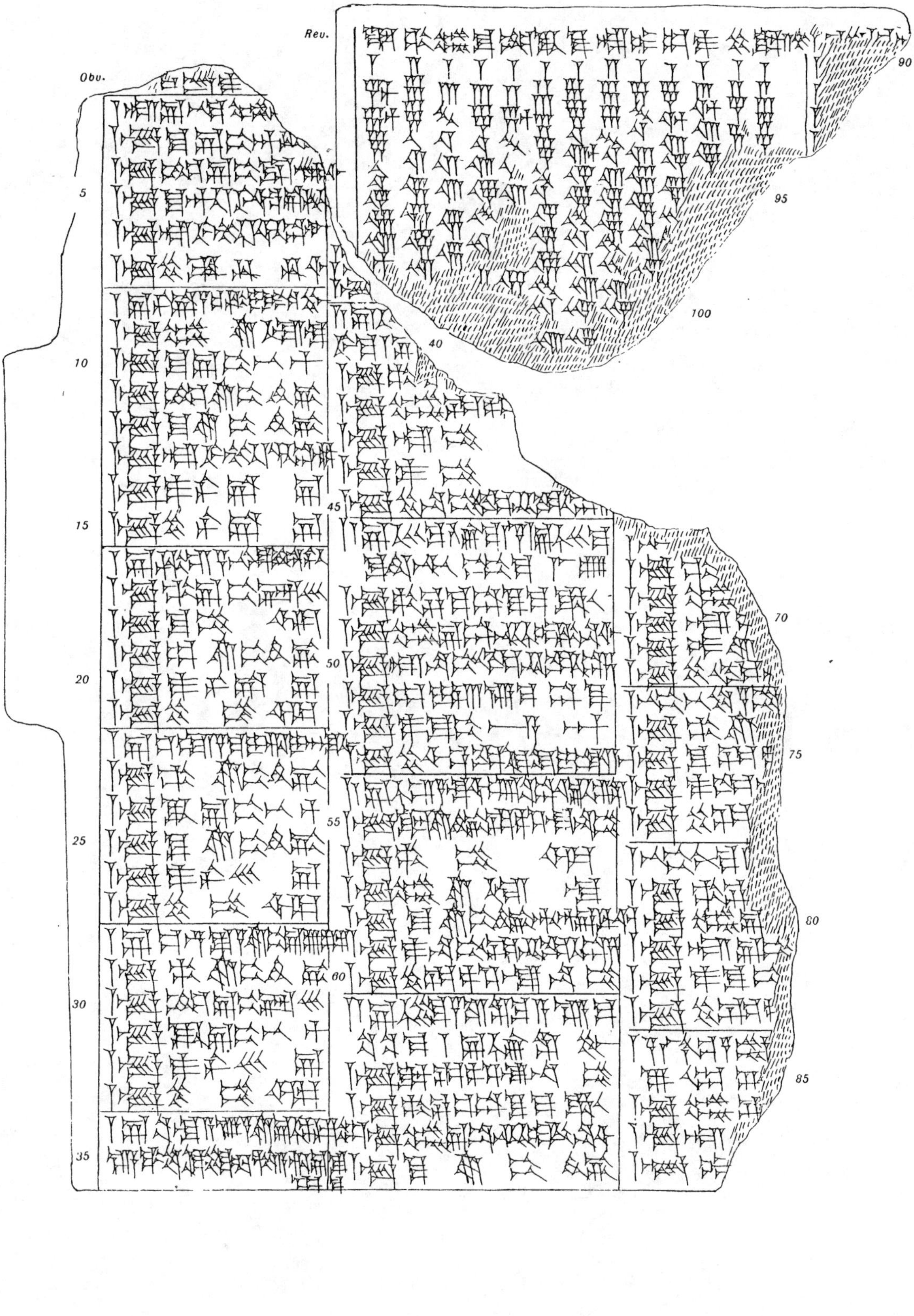

25

Obv.

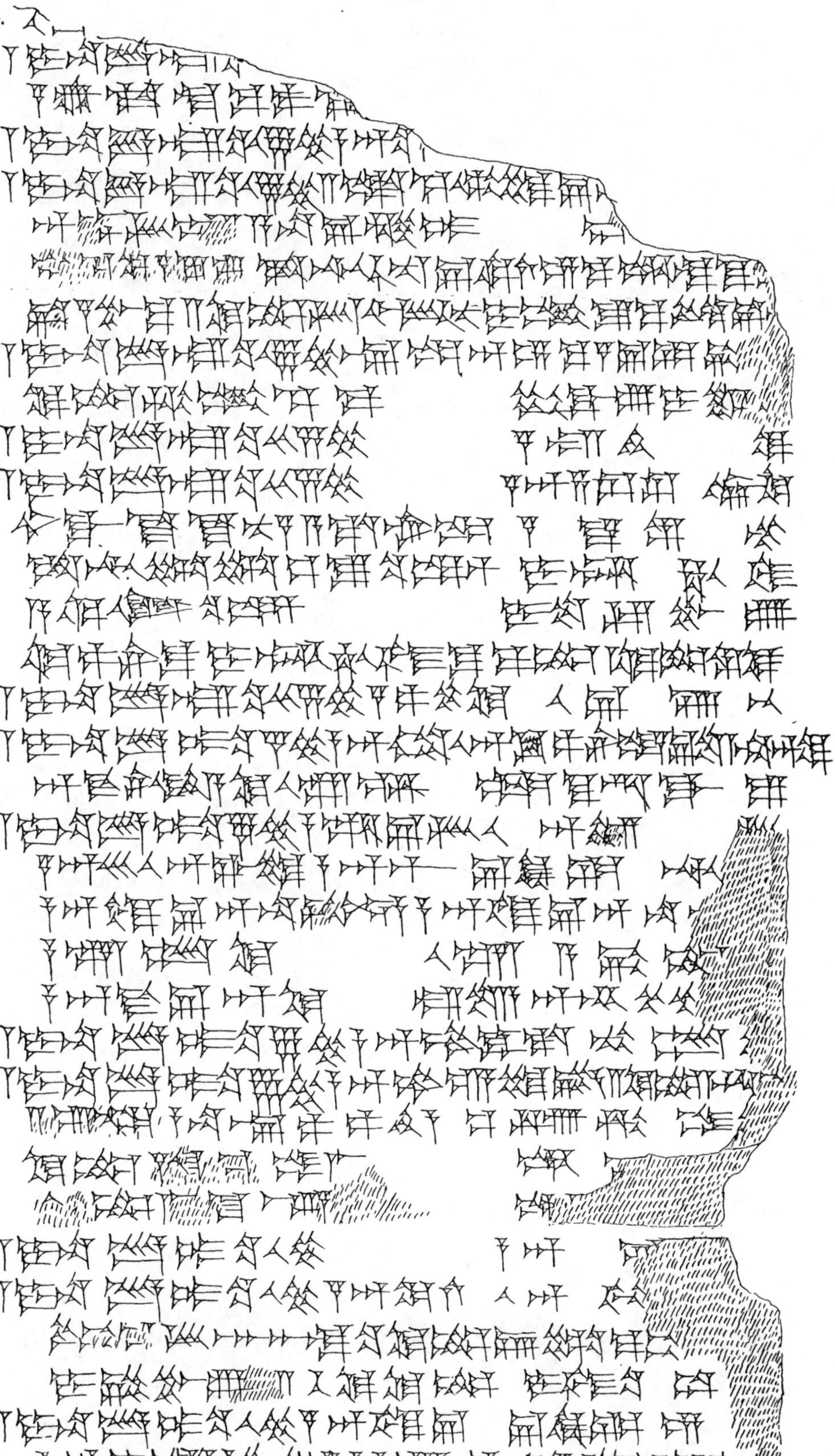

Rev.

25 CONTINUED

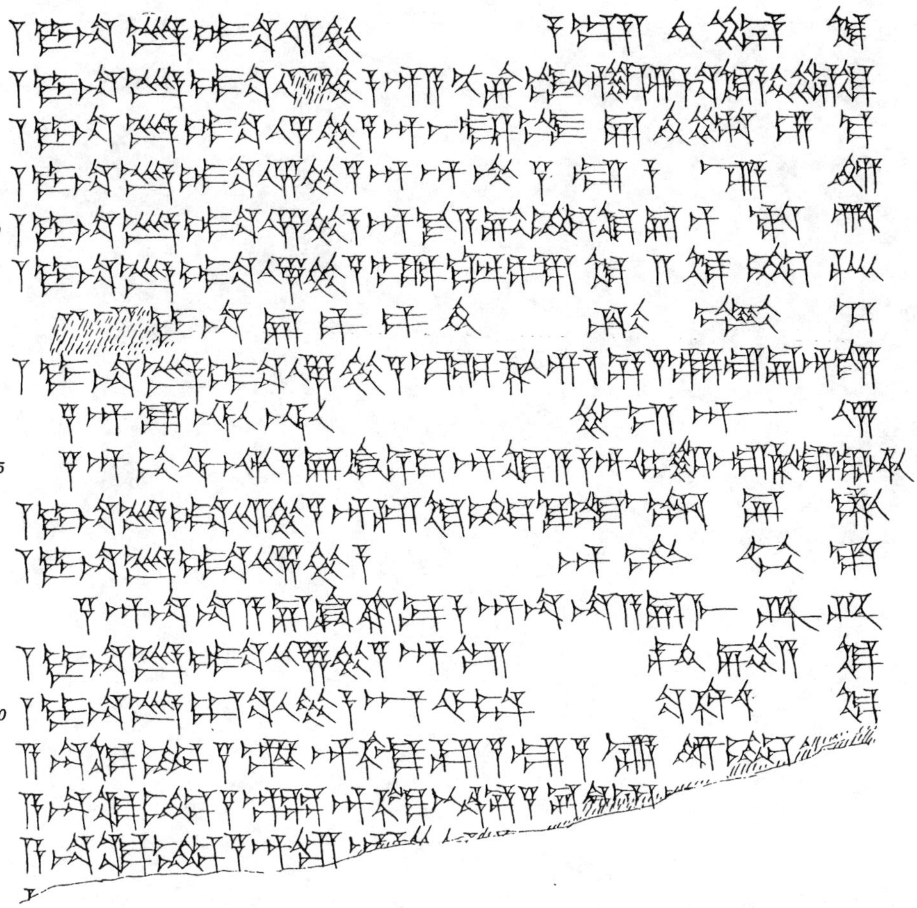

26

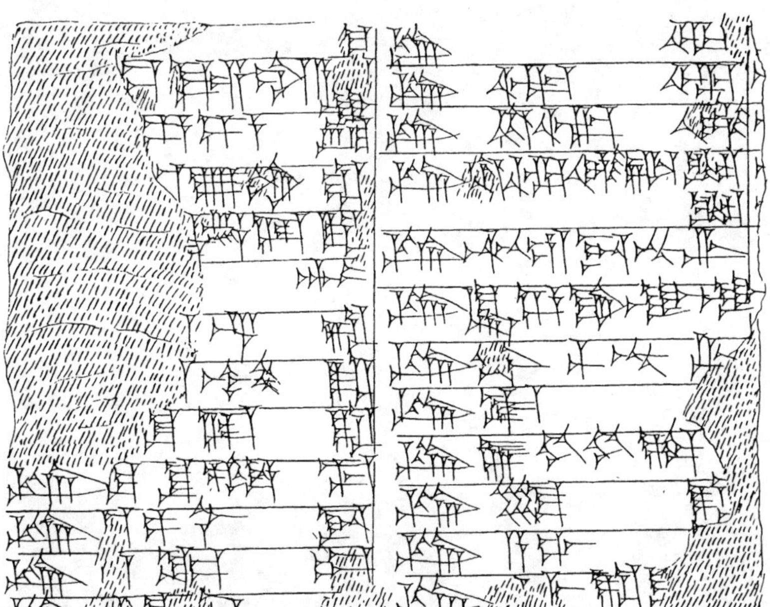

Rev.

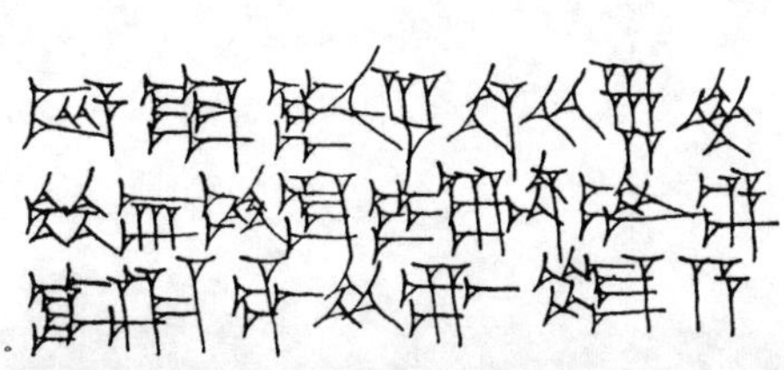

27

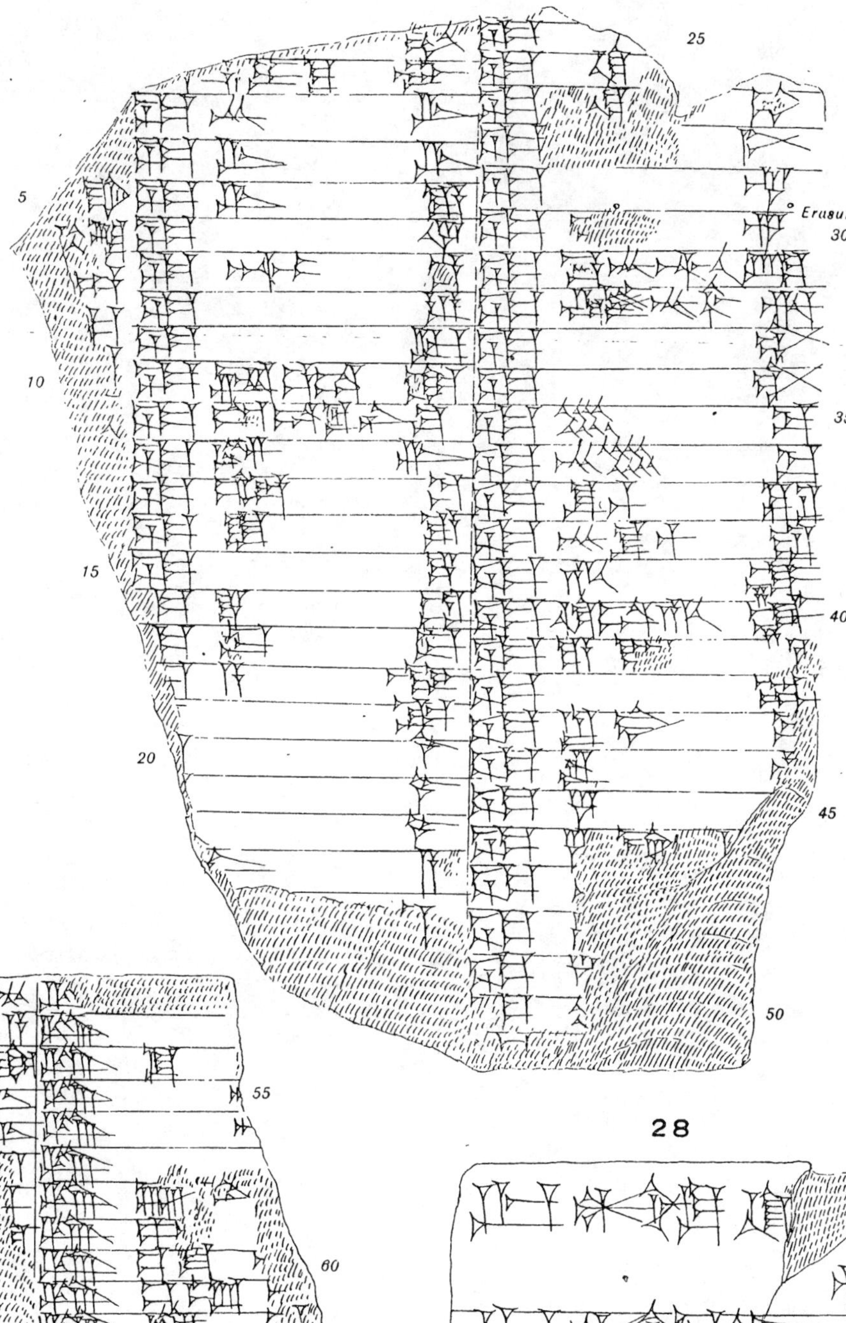

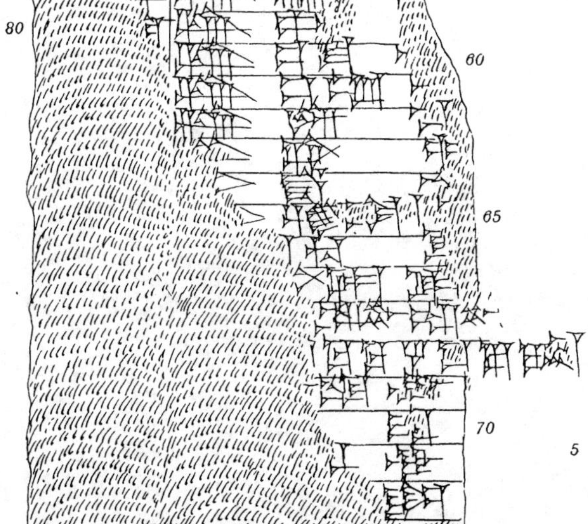

28

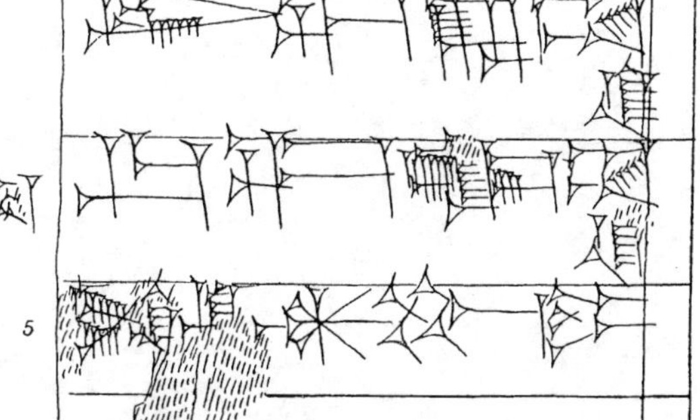

29

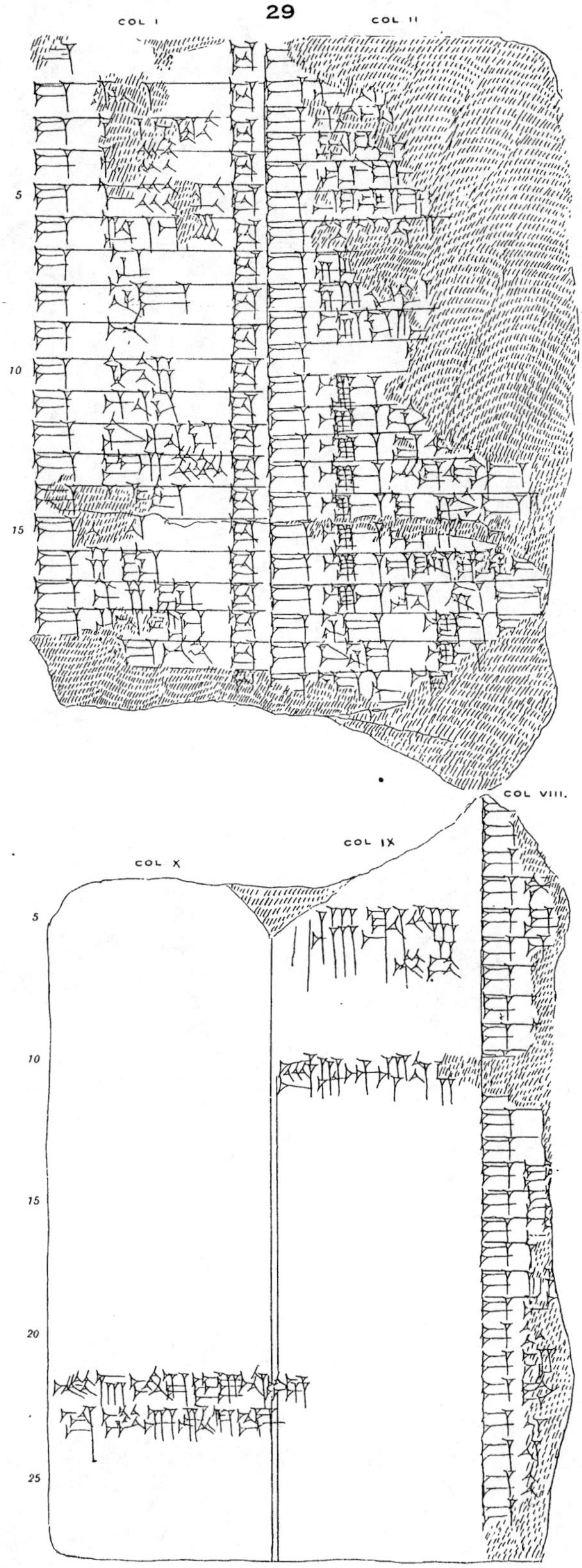

30

COL. IV. COL. V.

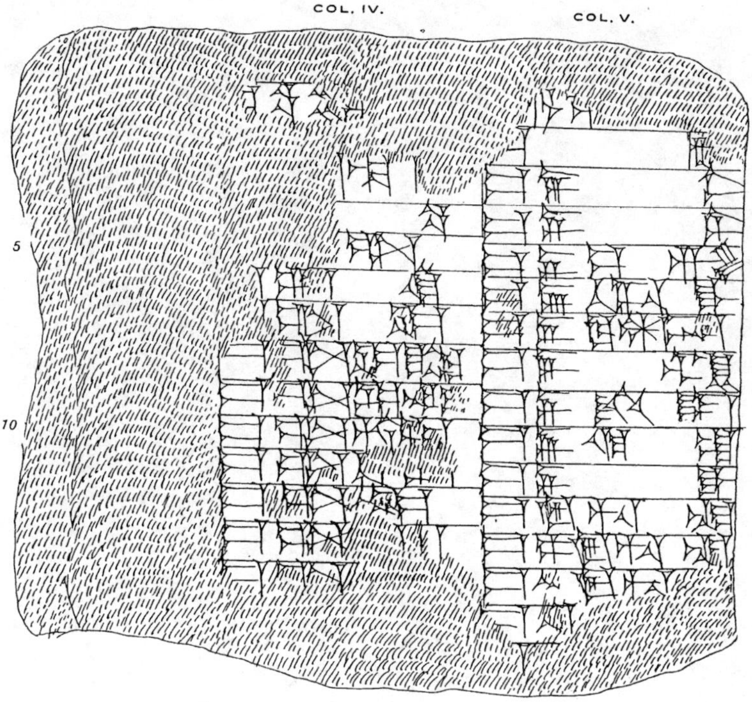

COL. VII. COL. VI.

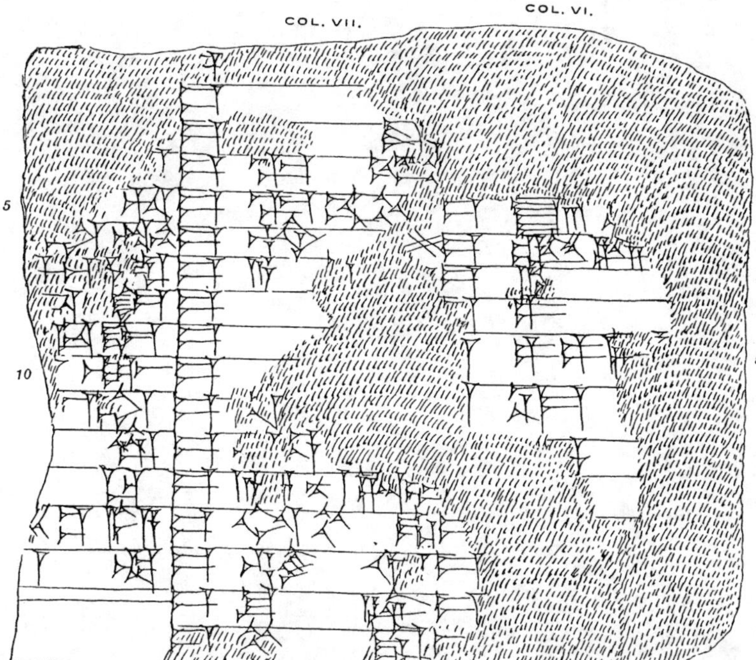

31

COL. I. COL. II.

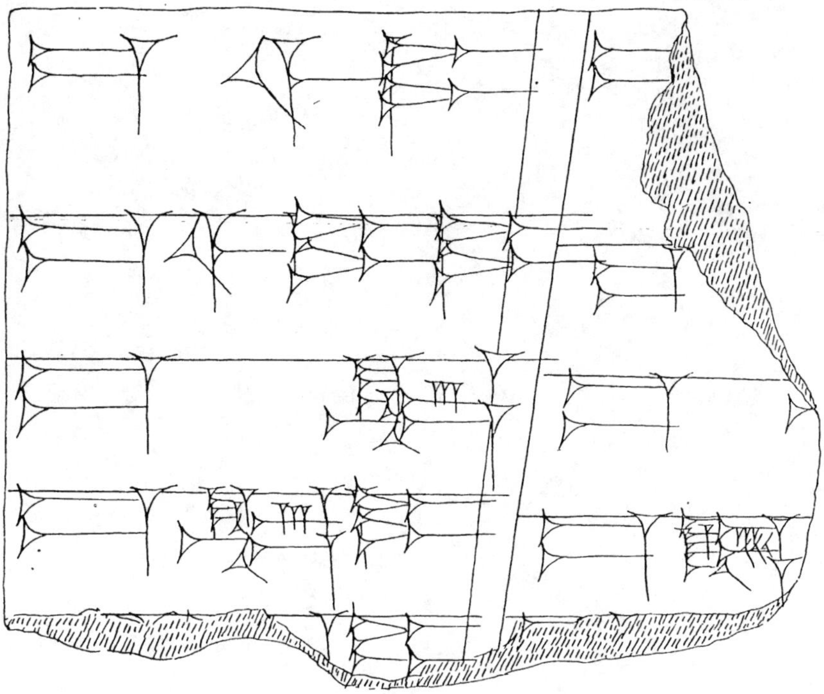

COL. VI. COL. V.

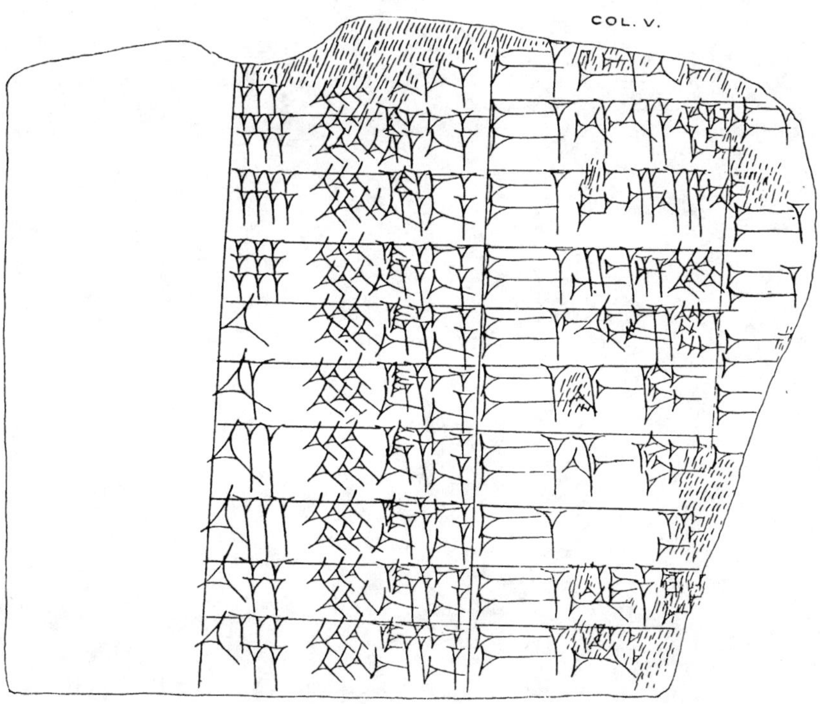

32

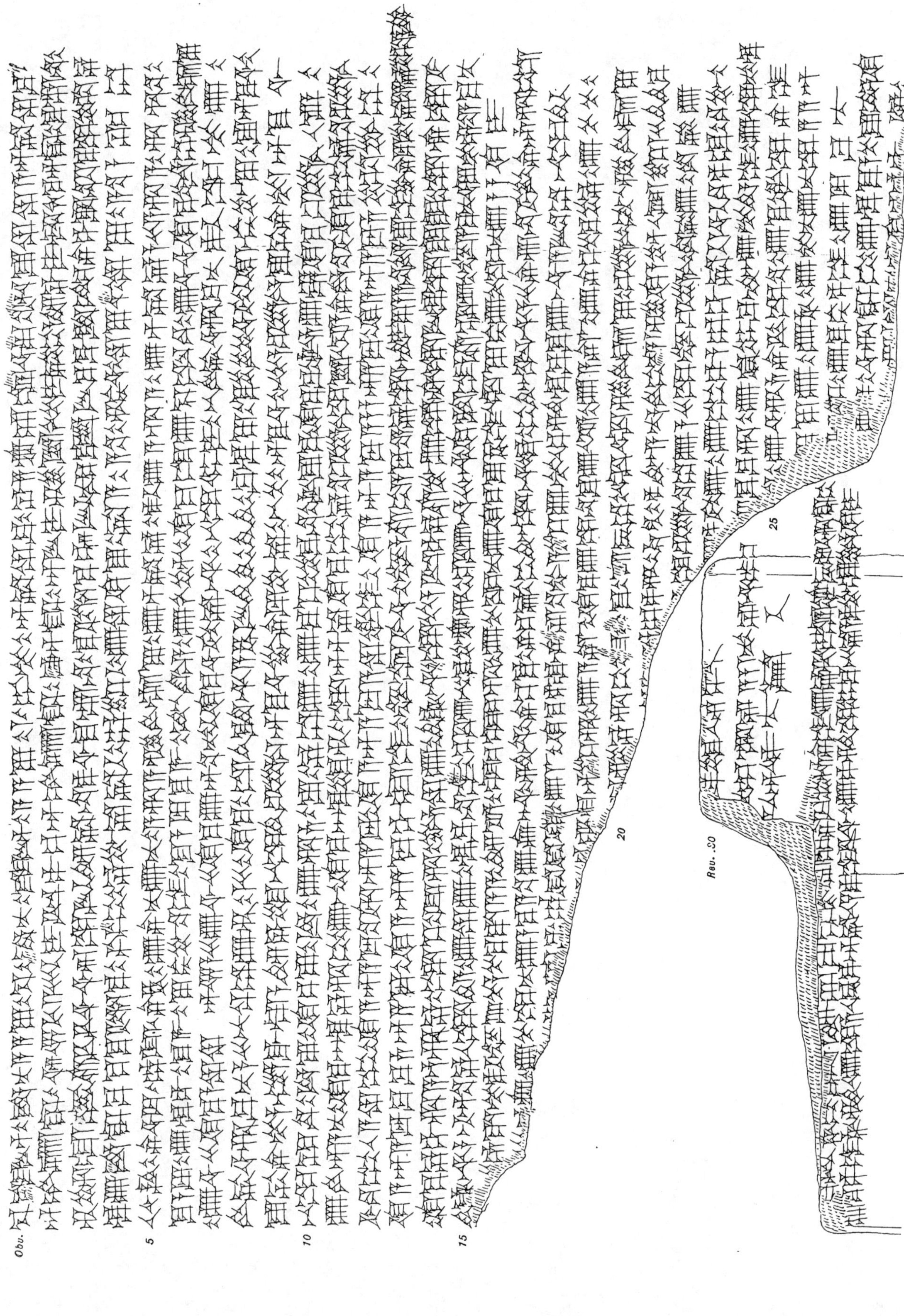

33

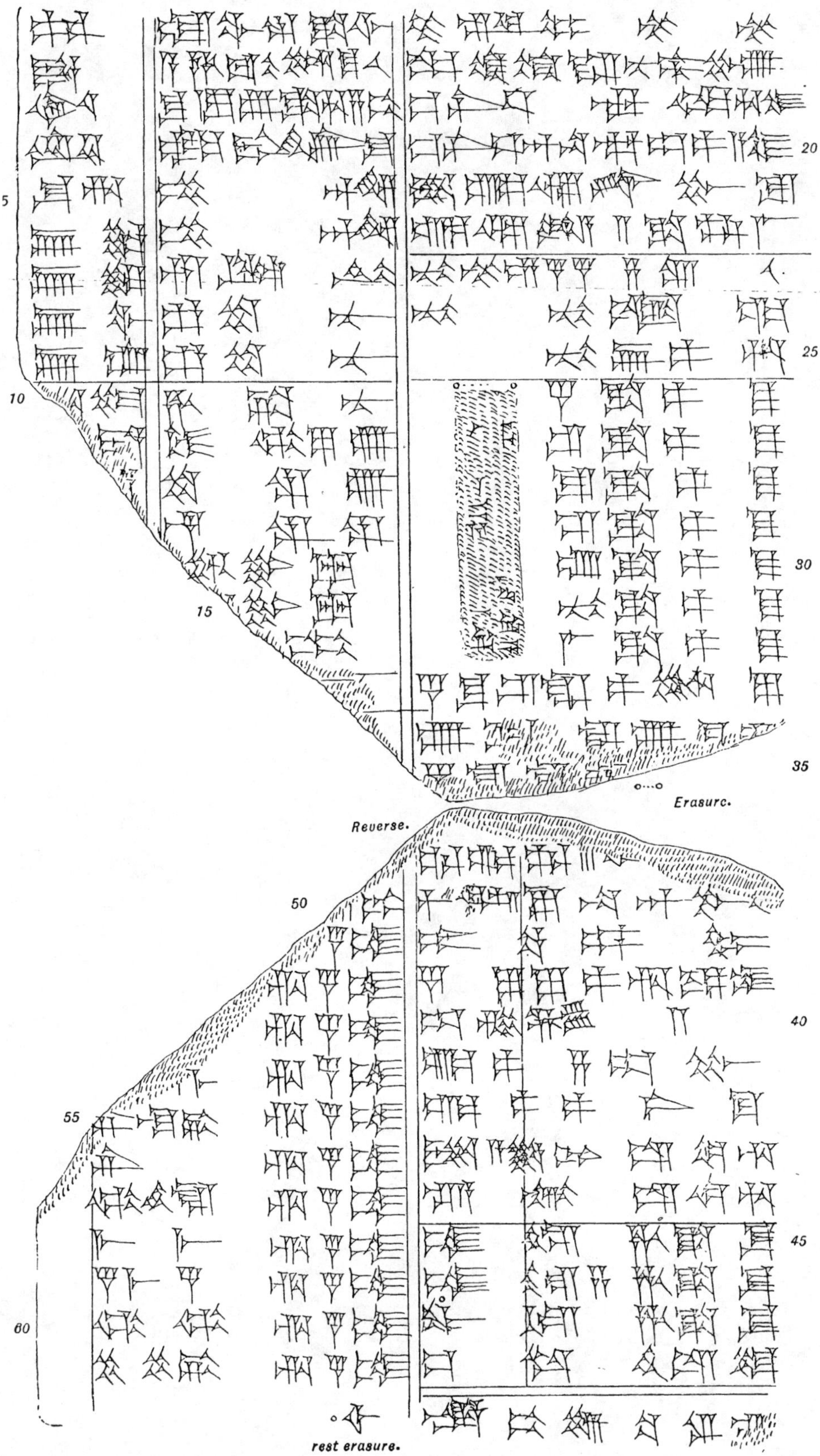

34

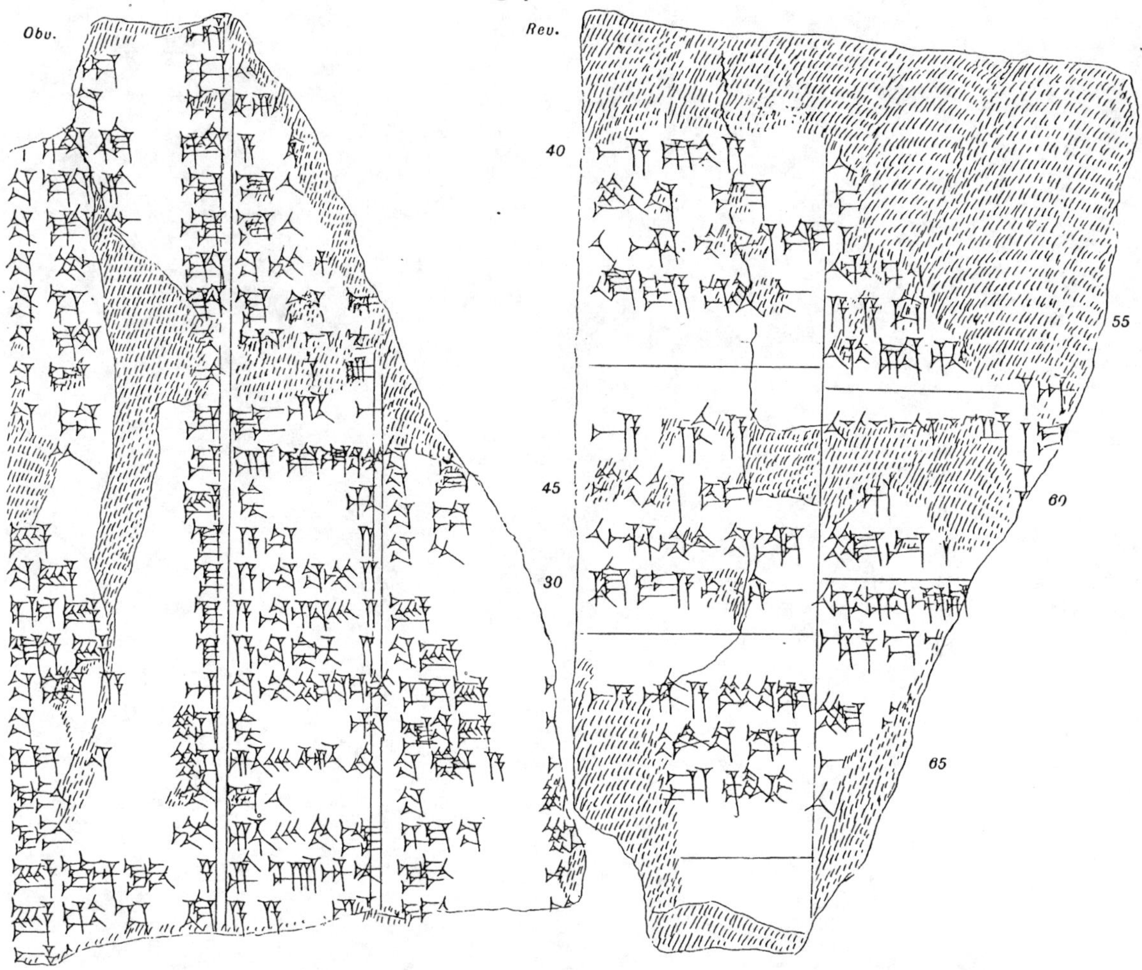

35

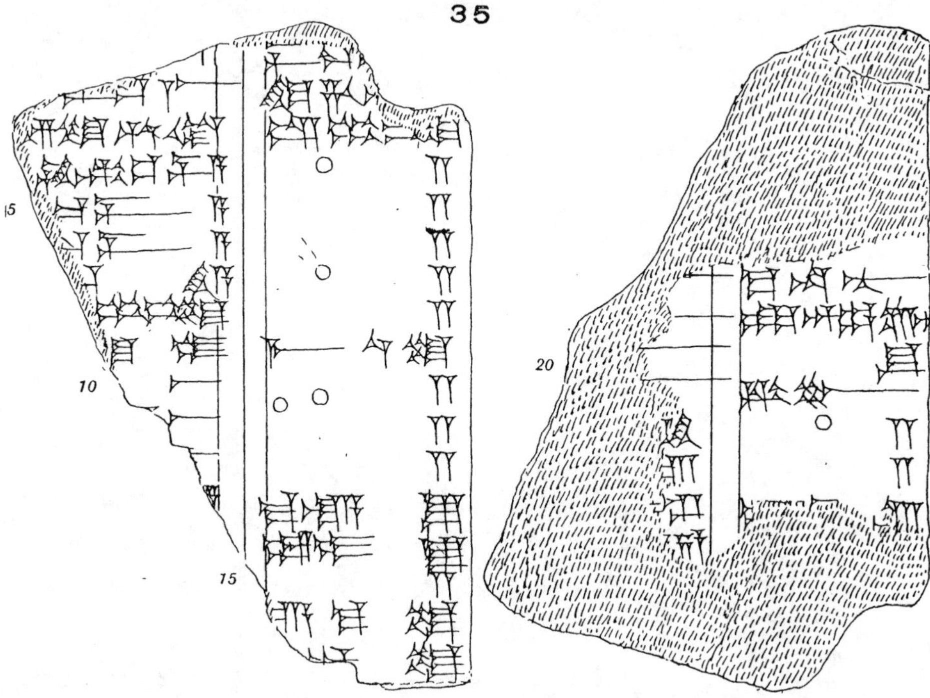

36

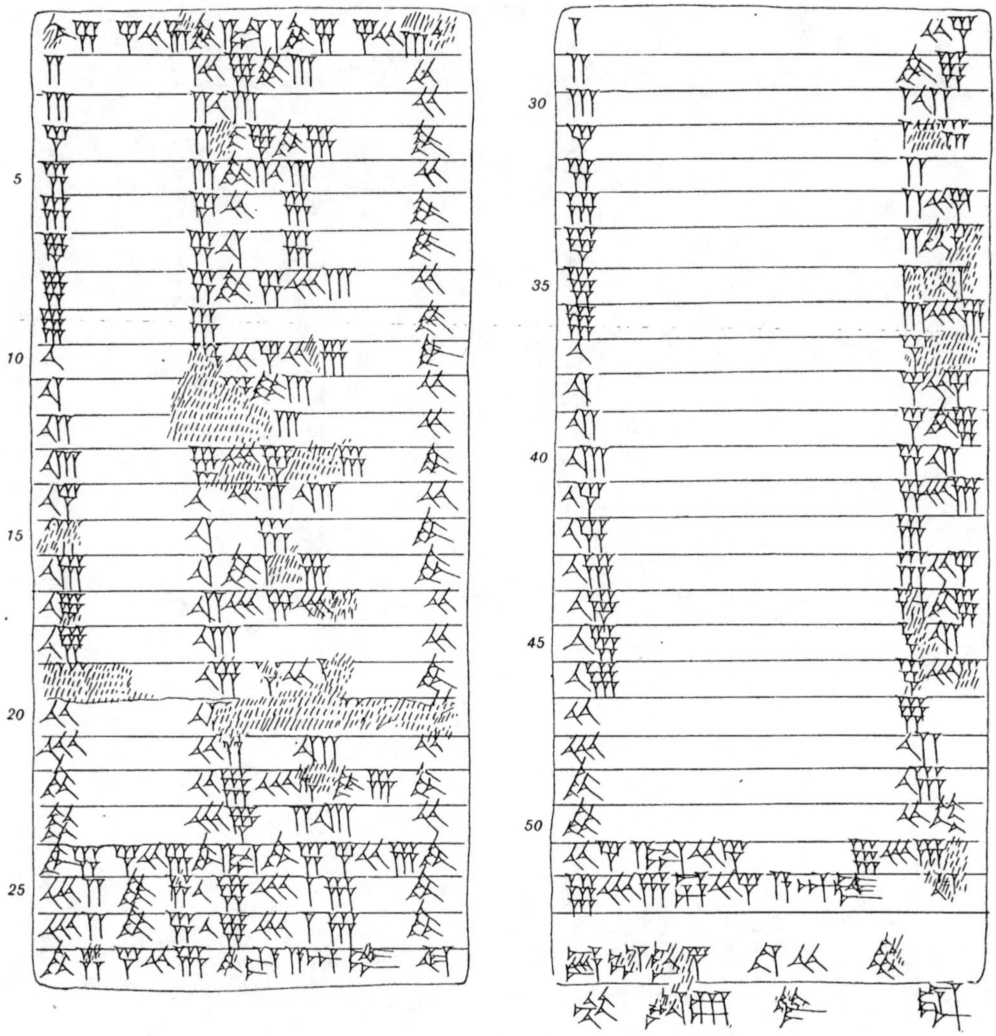

37

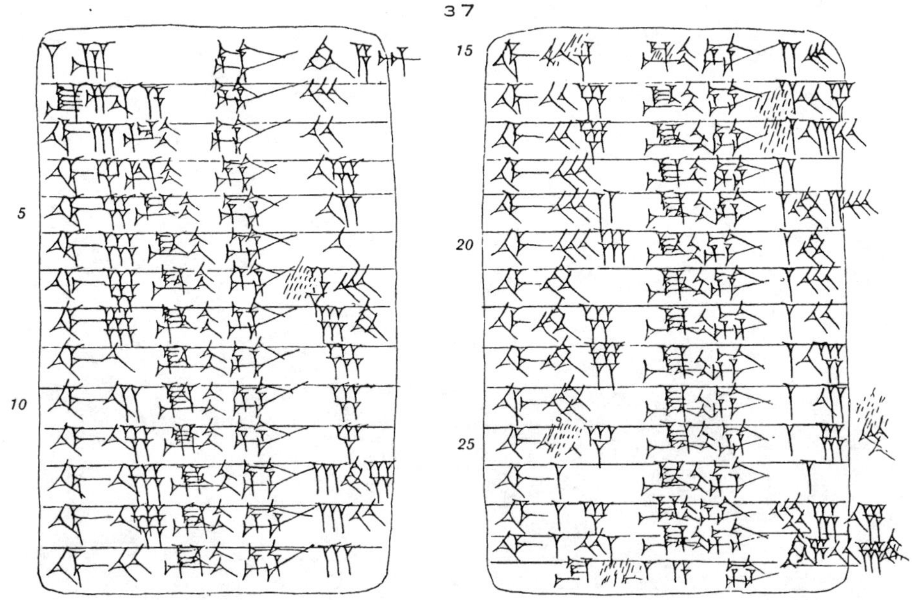

38

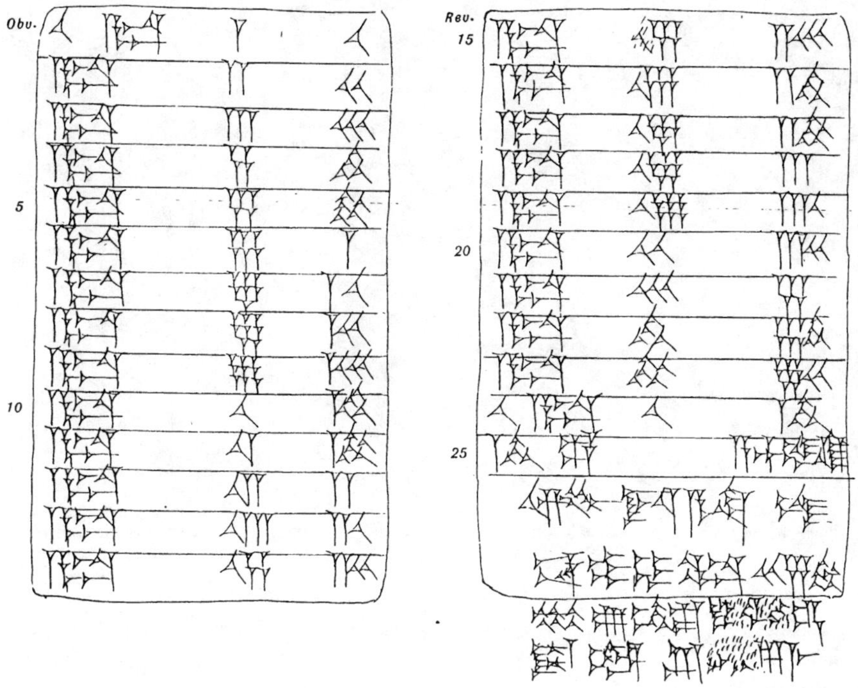

39

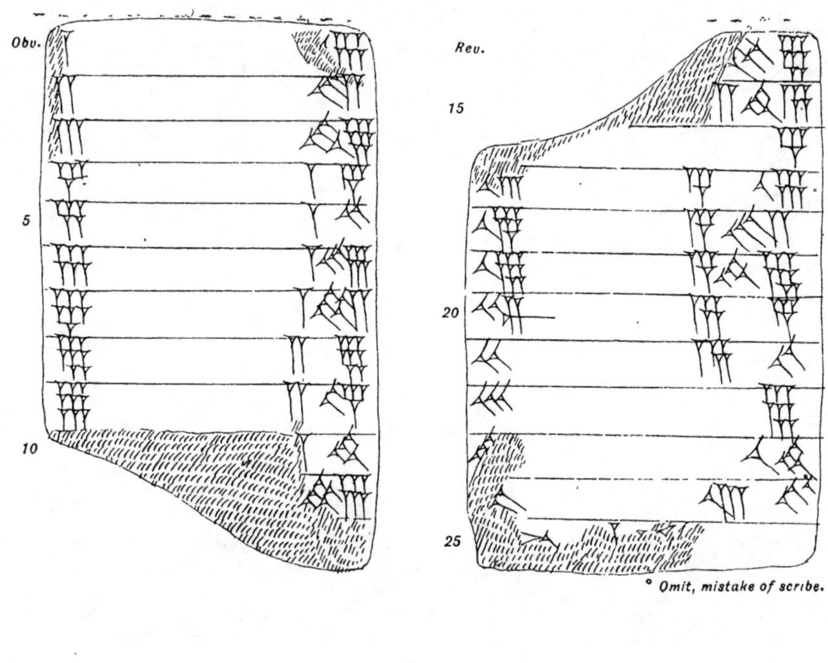

° Omit, mistake of scribe.

40

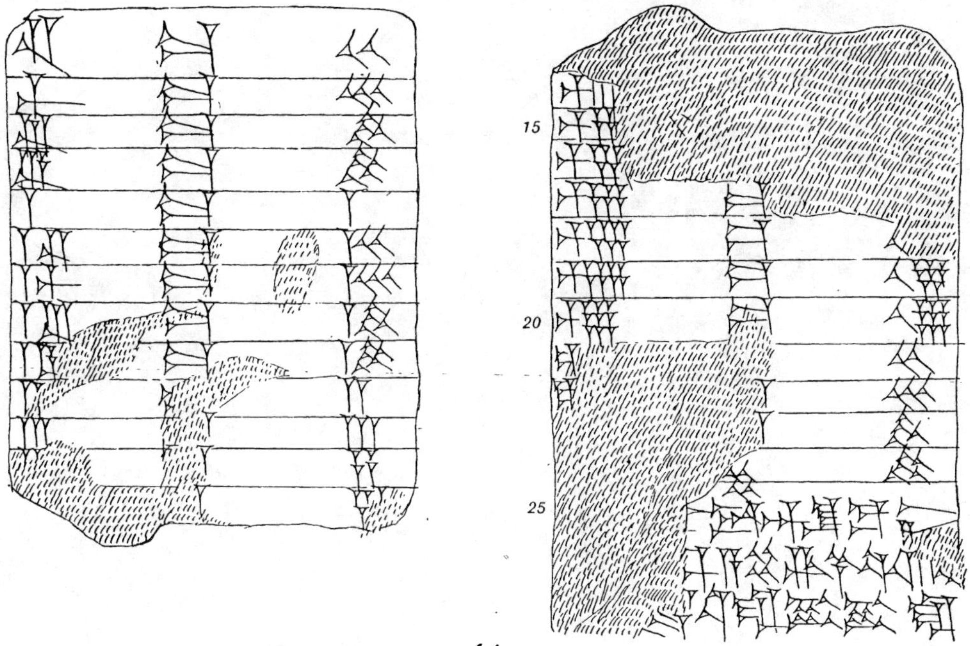

41

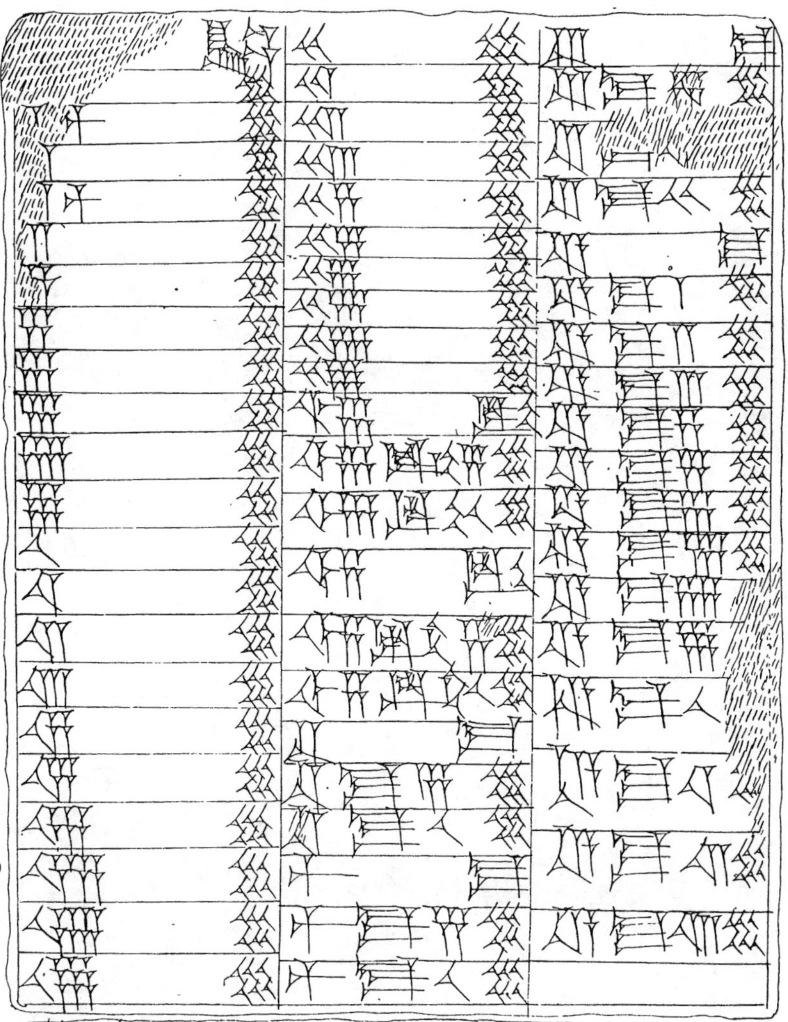

Lo. E.

41 CONTINUED

R.

U. E.

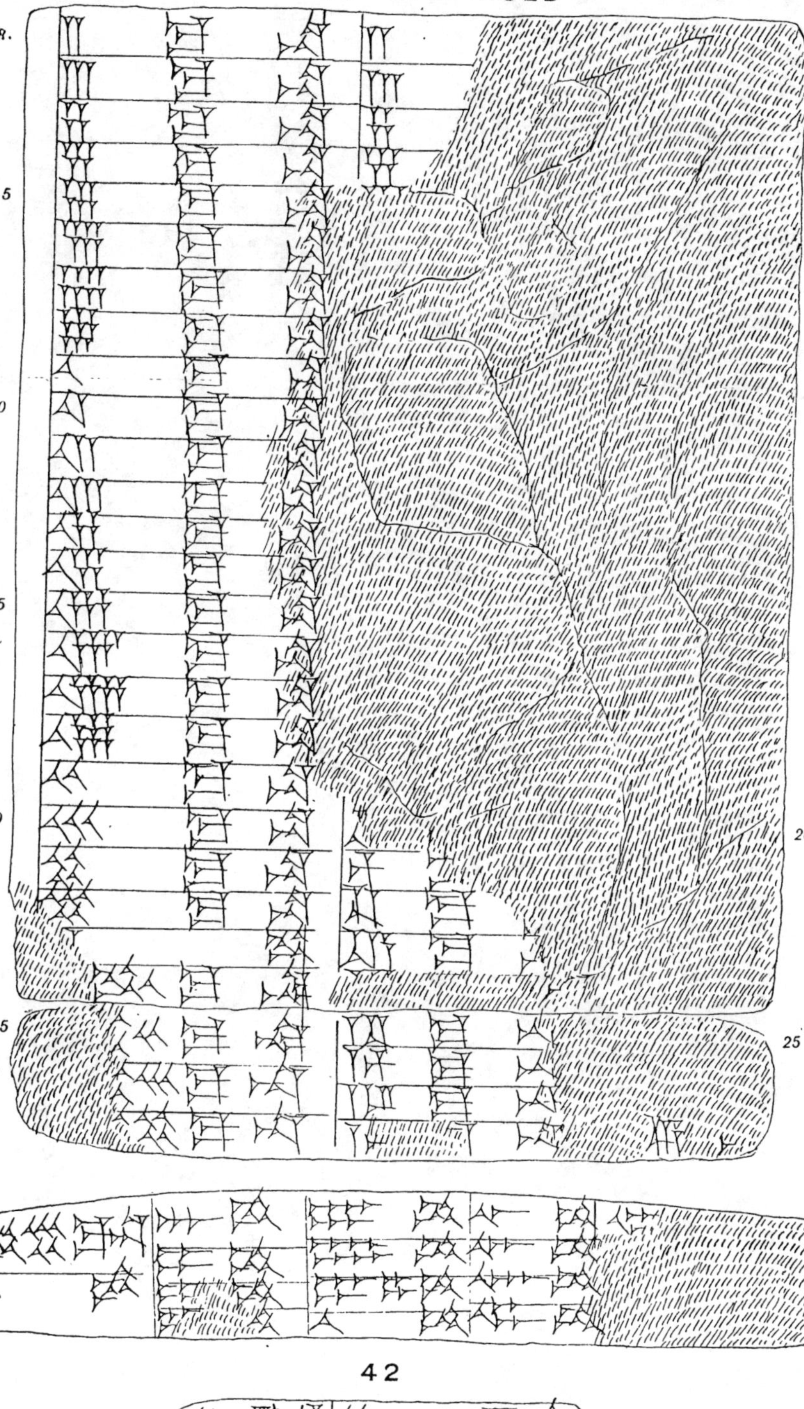

L. E.

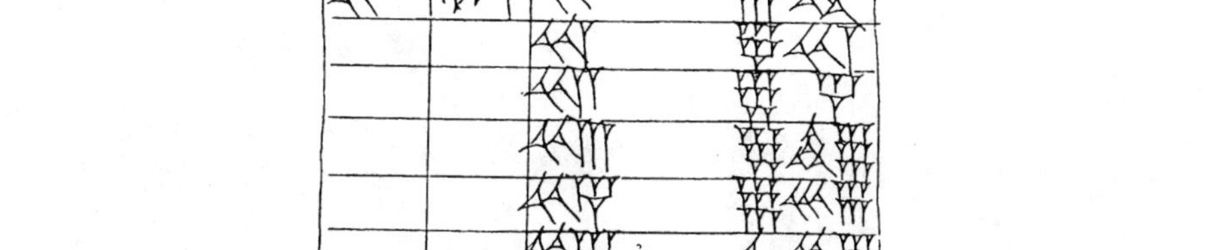

42

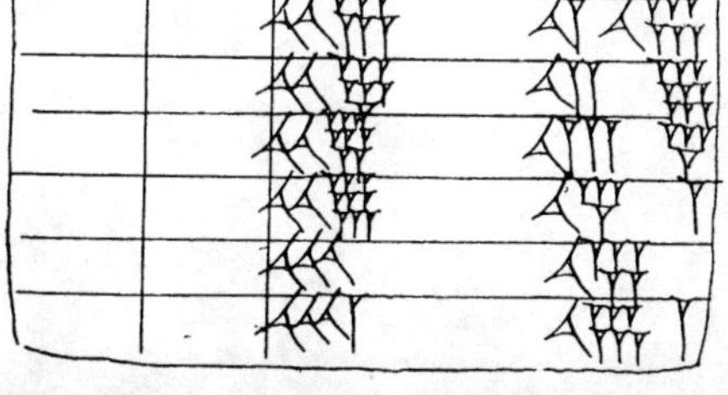

43

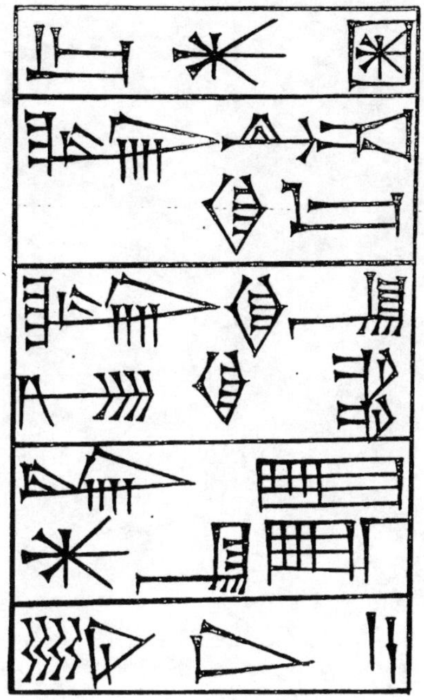

44

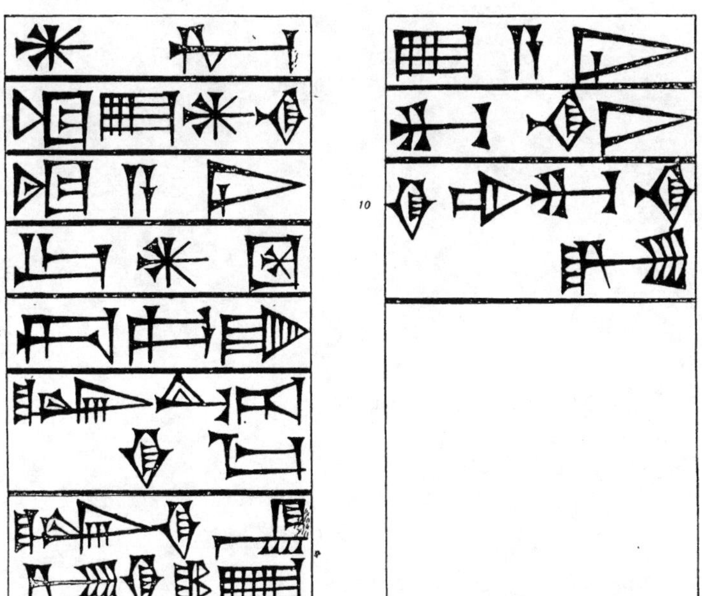

45

46

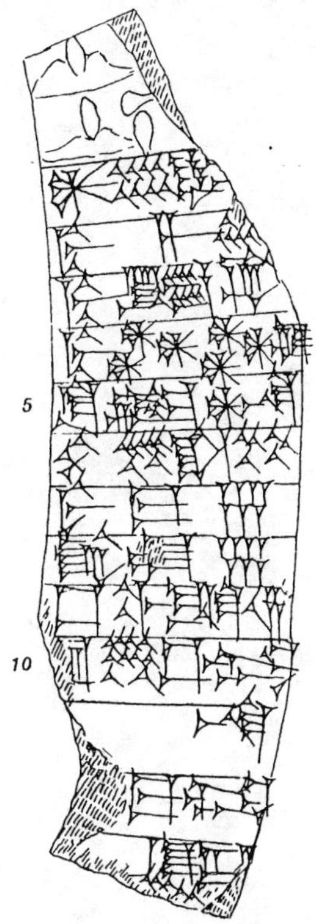

47

48

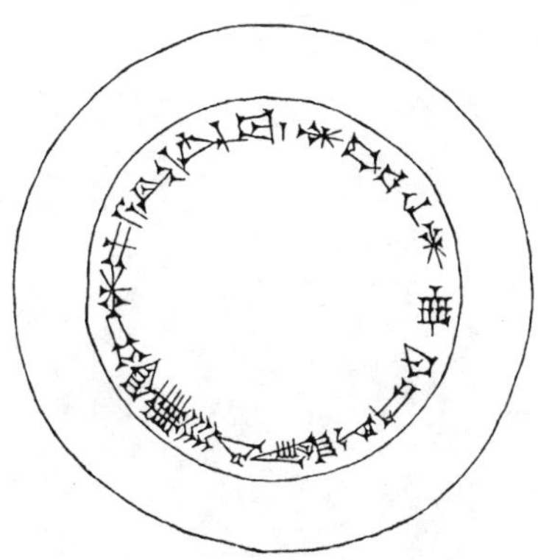

49

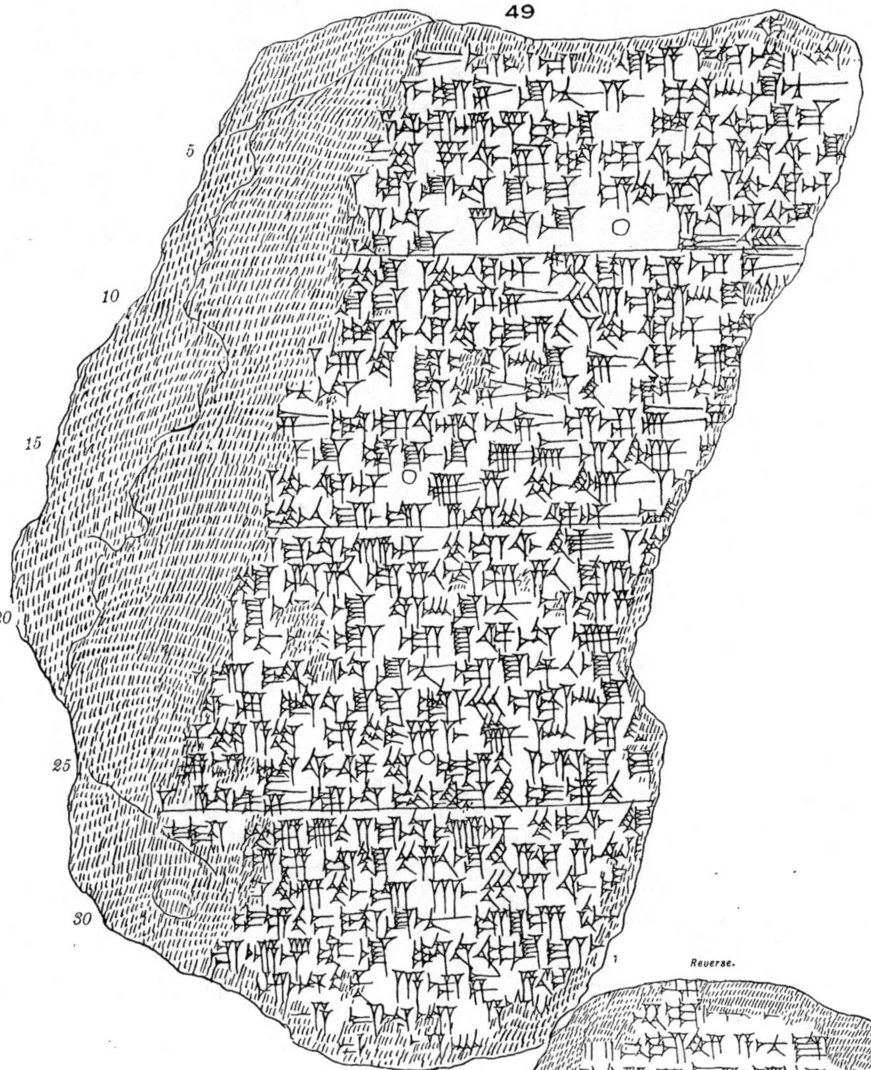

Reverse.

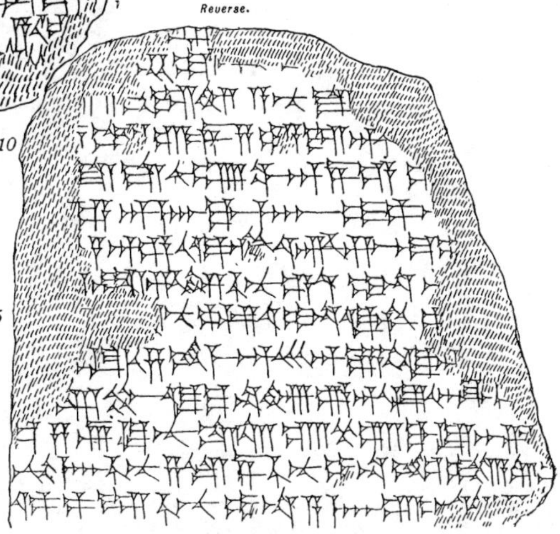

50

Obverse.

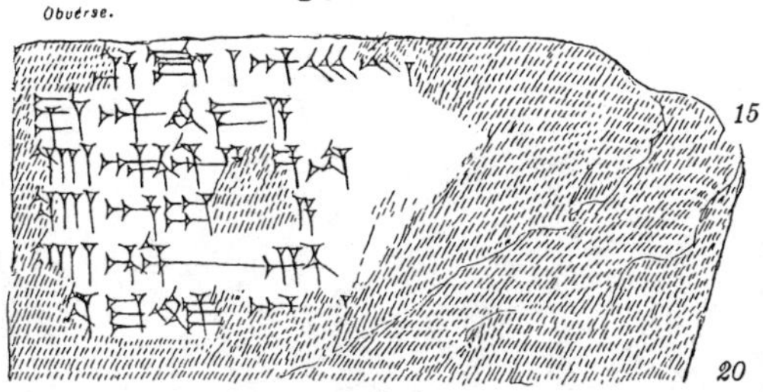

51

Col. I

Col. II

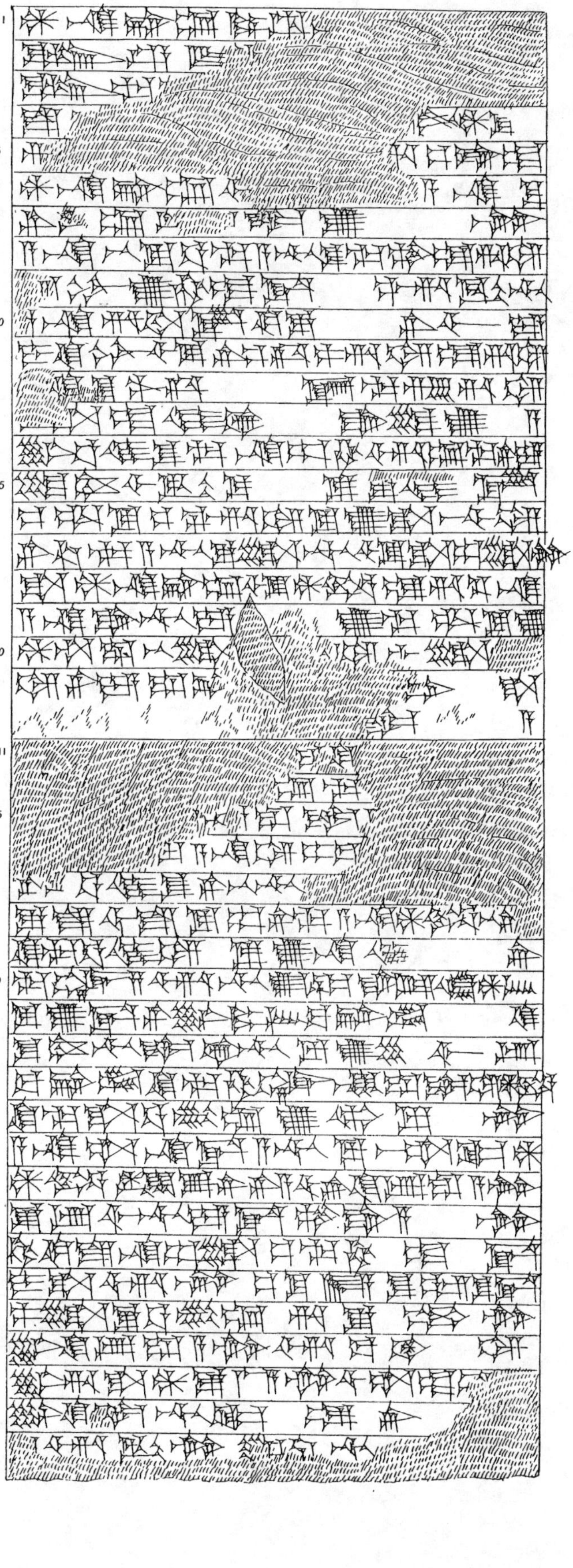

52

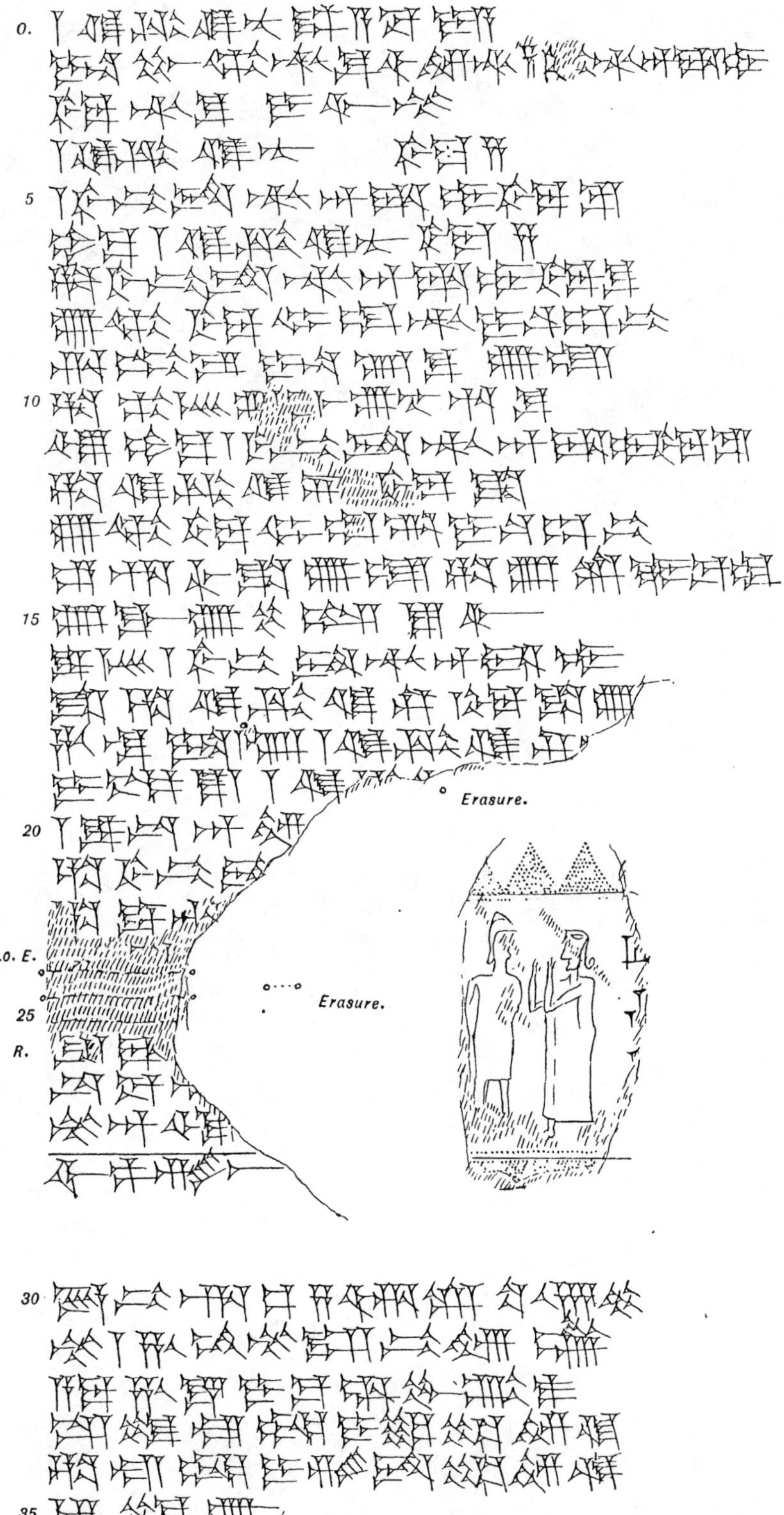

53

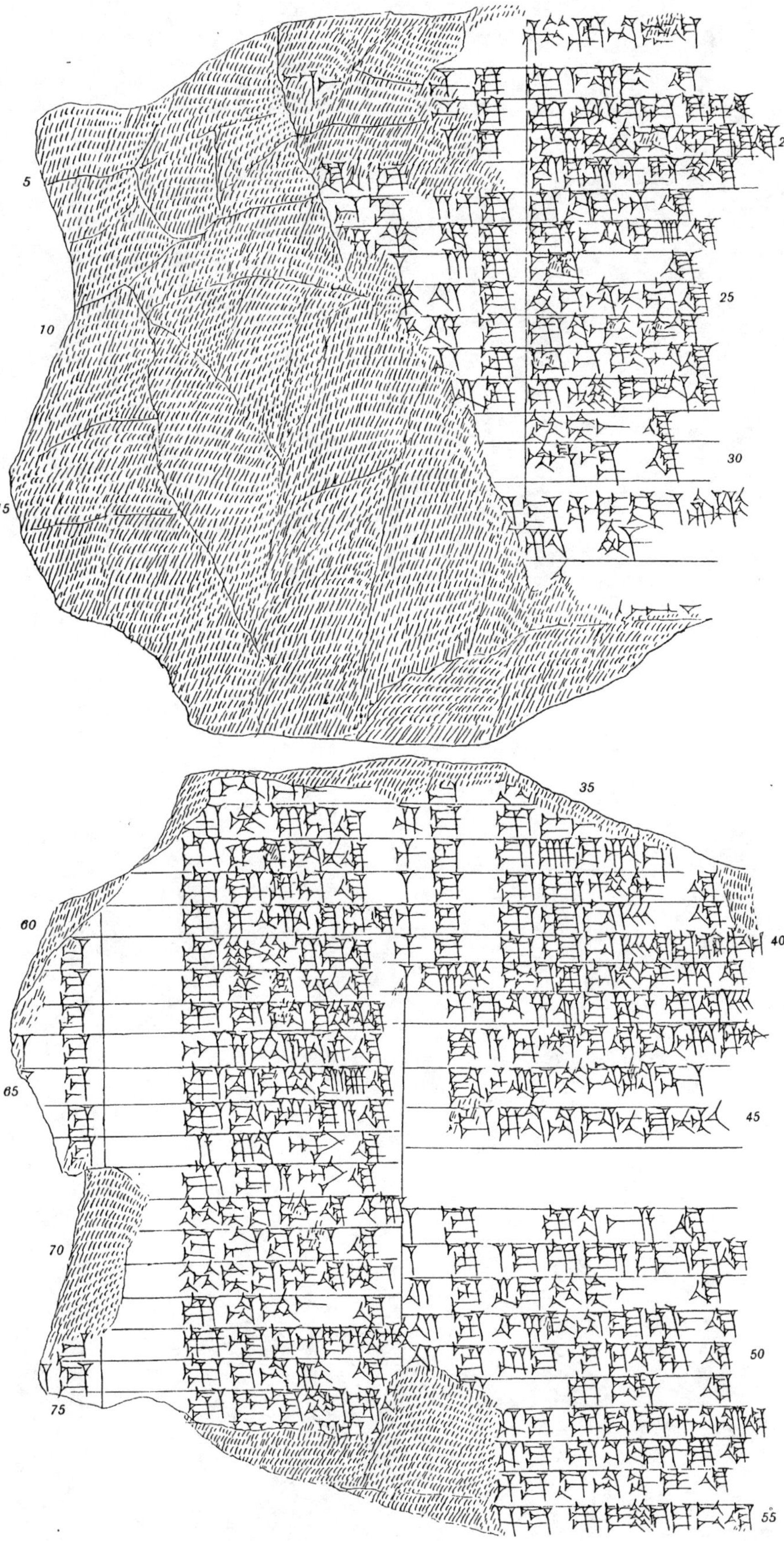

54

ΑΛΙΚΗ
Ο
ΡΧΩΝ

55

ΧΡΕΟΦΥΛΑ
ΟΡΧΩΝ

58

ΑΡΙϹΤΕΑϹ ωΙΑΜΟΟΝΟΜΑ
ΑΡΔΙΒΗΛΤΕΙΟϹ

56

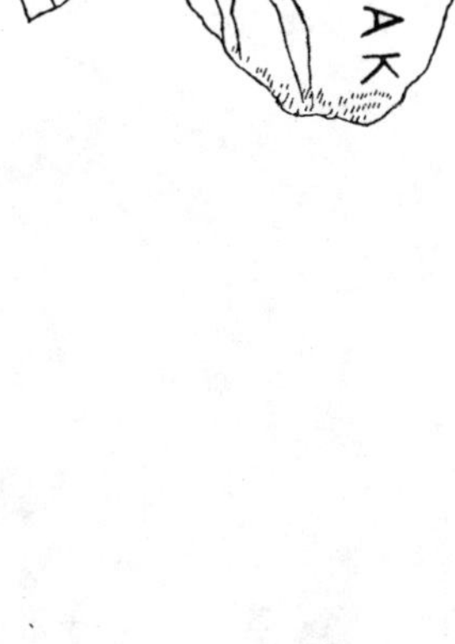
ΟΡΧΩ
ΥΛΑΚ

57

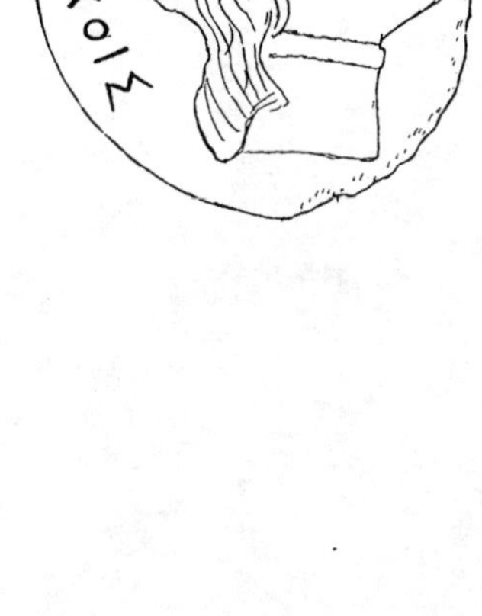
ΕΝΟΡΧΟΙΣ